HENRY VISCARDI, JR.

A MAN'S STATURE

Introduction by BERNARD M. BARUCH

THE JOHN DAY COMPANY

NEW YORK

To Lucile

Acknowledgment

This story is true, as I remember it.

Proper names, geographical locations, and circumstances have been altered in a few of the events recorded herein for the purpose of avoiding any embarrassment to the persons involved.

A mention of all those who have been part of this story and who have made J.O.B. possible would be so long as to be meaningless and incomplete, whatever its length. Thus I should like to acknowledge, if I may, the inspiration and generosity of the countless individuals who are contributing to the advancement of these efforts on behalf of the disabled worker.

I am most grateful to Orin Lehman, whose kindly devotion to this cause has been a source of inspiration and deep personal satisfaction for me and for all whom it has served.

I acknowledge my deepest gratitude to all those who have believed in this book and have helped make it possible, Richard J. Walsh, Mary Squire Abbot, Paul S. Eriksson, Mr. and Mrs. James Monahan, and Jean Nash.

H. V., Jr.

Introduction

Henry Viscardi was born under a cruel handicap. Most men would have been doomed by it to lives of misery and despair. He refused, however, to be consigned to humanity's scrap heap. He fought, with a courage that must fill the most impersonal heart with boundless admiration, to conquer the terrible disability and he won. Against great odds he made a normal life for himself. In that struggle he acquired a spirit which reflects his remarkable character.

Putting aside personal considerations, indeed at a sacrifice to them, he took up the task of opening the eyes of society to the needs of those who have suffered disabling afflictions. There are two million such of our fellow citizens, many of them veterans of our wars. They are men and women who want neither parades, pensions, nor pity. They want only a chance to work, to make their lives productive, to regain the dignity which idleness and a sense of uselessness destroys. Despite their disabilities they constitute a vast reservoir of skills, talents, and energies. They are one of the great but neglected resources of the land. Society does itself a disservice, even in an economic sense, by its reluctance to employ these willing and able hands. It wrongs itself by failing to

tap the great spiritual resources of these people, resources
which have been refined and tempered in adversity.

Those who have wavered beneath physical and spiritual
affliction will find inspiration in Henry Viscardi's life. Those
who too often lose themselves in the petty complaints of
everyday life will be moved to re-evaluate their problems
after reading this book.

A Man's Stature will open understanding hearts and helping hands to a noble cause. It will also reveal the stature of
Henry Viscardi.

BERNARD M. BARUCH

Contents

A Man's Stature

1

Home

I liked the hospital. It was my home.

First of all there was Gouldie. She didn't wear a white uniform like the nurses. She was the "kindergarten teacher." She smelled like flowers all the time and she had silvery hair. One day she brought a bowl of water to my bedside table and helped me sail paper boats in it.

Then there was Dr. Frauenthal. He was straight and tall, and I trusted him. He had a long red beard. Later when I saw a picture of Moses I realized that he looked like Dr. Frauenthal, except that Moses had more hair on top.

When Dr. Frauenthal came through the ward with his long white coat swaying, some younger doctors walked a few steps behind him. They listened when he tapped my cast with his forefinger and explained to them about the new feet he was making for me, and they watched while he did something to the weights that hung at the end of my bed. Dr. Frauenthal didn't call me "Cardy" as Gouldie did, and he hardly ever laughed. I knew that every time I was taken to the operating room or was put into splints or traction Dr. Frauenthal was to blame. But I still liked him.

And there was George. He wore a white apron and a tall white cap. He was the biggest man and he had the whitest teeth and the blackest skin and the nicest smile of anybody I ever saw. He was bigger even than Dr. Frauenthal. And he could make the best baked macaroni in the whole world.

There was somebody called Your Father who came to see me on Sundays and brought presents. Sometimes he brought rice cakes that he said were made by a Chinese man. And once he came with a big bowl of strawberries. He didn't wear a white coat, just a suit. He would stand and look at me for a while and say, "How's my boy? Pretty good, eh?"

The hospital was a nice place because I could have everything I wanted. There were toys to play with and books and Teddy bears. If I wanted a drink of water, I called to the nurse and she brought it to me. If I was cold she covered me up. Lots of times I had ice cream—every day I guess. On warm days they moved me out on the porch and I could look down and watch children playing in the park across the street. Sometimes they danced around a tall pole with long ribbons on it.

One day when I was showing Gouldie a picture of George that I had colored with crayons, she said, "That's good, Cardy." Then she looked at a woman who had just come in. "Did you know you're going to have a visitor today?"

Visitors were big people. They said things like "Who's this sweet little boy?" When they came to see me it meant that I had to stop coloring and I couldn't talk to Gouldie any more. Visitors asked me questions and they never stopped talking.

Gouldie showed me how to make things and sometimes she held me on her lap and told me stories and sometimes she didn't talk at all. She just smiled at me as though she understood everything—even the things I wanted to say but didn't know the words for.

"I don't want any visitors!" I whined.

"It's Your Mother," she said.

I looked at the woman with the big brown eyes. She stood by the foot of my bed and she didn't say anything—she just looked at me. What did she want?

Then I knew. She had come to take me away and I would never see Gouldie again, ever. I grabbed Gouldie's wrists and buried my face in her smock.

"Don't go away, don't go away," I wailed.

Gouldie raised my head and wiped my eyes with her handkerchief.

The woman was still standing by my bed and she smiled. But she smiled in a strange way as if she might cry any minute.

It was not surprising that I did not know my mother, because most of the first six years of my life were spent in the hospital in the care of doctors and nurses, and she rarely had the opportunity to visit me.

I was born on May 10, 1912, with underdeveloped legs. This was a great shock to my family, particularly since my parents were both normal and they had already had one perfectly normal baby girl.

My condition, in medical terminology, was described as "arrested development of the lower limbs resulting in incomplete growth of the bones and spasticity of the immature, ill-formed muscles." My short thighs ended in two small stumps twisted across each other on the abdomen. In the right limb there was a kneecap, imperfect but sufficient to allow for motion. Below that was a small mass of tissue containing two inadequate pieces of bone, a rudimentary tibia and fibula. From this hung what should have been a foot, with three small nodes of flesh for toes. The left limb was worse: it lacked both the kneecap and the "foot." And both legs were tightly enfolded by the muscle pull so that they could not be straightened without severe pain and without reverting immediately to the original position on release.

My case was not unique. The answer to why a child is born this way lies in the fact that at some time during the mother's pregnancy the cells designated to become legs stop developing in the normal way. It could happen to any part of the body with even more serious results, depending upon which cells are affected.

During my babyhood, neighborhood doctors prescribed various forms of treatment. One bandaged me to a board with the center cut out—this served as a giant splint. Another cut a tendon in an attempt to straighten what there was of my foot.

My mother, being a religious person, decided that it would not hurt to seek supplementary spiritual aid. Almost immediately after I was born she dedicated me to St. Anthony. As soon as she was able, she made a visit to St. Anthony's Church, which was a long distance from the part of New York City in which she lived. She bought miniature limbs of wax at a store and placed them on the saint's altar in accordance with the Old World custom that her people had brought to this country. And she prayed to him that her son would some day have legs and be able to walk. She made a promise then which she has faithfully kept by taking flowers to her own church every year in June on the feast day of St. Anthony, even when she has picked the flowers herself rather than buy them.

It was the best deal Mamma ever made. St. Anthony kept his part of the bargain.

But it took twenty-five years.

Before I was two years old I was admitted to the Hospital for Deformities and Joint Diseases on New York's upper east side. Dr. Frauenthal began a long series of operations and treatments which were to last four years. The expense involved in such medical care could not have been met by an immigrant Italian family such as mine. My father, who was a barber, had his own shop, but the business probably did not provide more than an adequate living for Mamma and us children—and some help for his own mother who was a widow. Although I am not certain, I believe that a well-to-do patron of Papa's provided in large part for my hospitalization.

Every Sunday my family came to the hospital, but since child visitors were not allowed, my mother stayed across the street in Mt. Morris Park with my older sister Terry and let my father come inside to see me. Later, after Lillian was born, Mamma was busy at home caring for her young family. One summer she found a flat near the hospital. Then when she discovered that her hurried visits only upset me because I did not really know her, she stopped coming. Sometimes she watched me from the park when I was out on the porch, but she hid behind a tree so that I would not see her.

Dr. Frauenthal's first problem was to straighten the legs. This was done by a succession of operations through which the short tight muscles were lengthened and held in position with casts and splints.

At the age of three I was the "oldest resident" in the children's ward. Other patients came and left—wearing braces and casts, waving good-by as they limped out on crutches or walked on good solid legs that had been mended. But I stayed. It seemed as though I had always been there.

I had three ordeals. First, the repeated trips to the operating room with the frightening lights and the suffocation of the anesthetic. Then there was traction, or the heavy weights that kept pulling me toward the bottom of the bed. They were always there and I could not win. The other ordeal, which replaced the traction at intervals, was steel splints.

They clamped down over my right "foot" like the jaws of an L-shaped trap. When they were removed, the pain would disappear and the blessed cool air would touch my skin. Then back to the hard pull of the traction.

After my limbs were reasonably straight, Dr. Frauenthal began a series of operations to fuse the bones and create an area in both limbs which would bear the body weight. By the time I was four he had me getting around in a pair of casts.

As I grew stronger and learned to walk in these stiff leggings, I began to explore the ward. When the ward was full there were lots of children to visit and trade toys with. There were some very small babies who slept all the time and some who cried all the time. They had little beds with bars on the side. I had graduated from one of these. There were big boys and girls whose beds did not need to have sides. And there were boys and girls who were in casts. Sometimes they had their arms or legs fastened to pulleys that hung over their beds.

My bed was wonderful. The foot of it was really a fireman's ladder, which I learned to shinny up and down in time of emergency. One day I fell—overcome by smoke probably—but I came to, violently, when I hit the floor. My head was bleeding, but my howls brought a rescue squad on the double with bandages and adhesive tape. I still have the scar.

Finally the casts were replaced by leather orthopedic boots. The left one was built up on the inside with cork in the places where there was no foot. The right boot, which was larger, also had cork padding, but not so much. They only resembled shoes by the furthest stretch of the imagination, but they supported my body weight. What did it matter if my feet were not parallel when I took steps? With the boots on I could walk and I could run.

I could go practically anywhere. Also I discovered that because I was barely two feet tall I could go places that nobody else could. I could walk under my bed, and I could hide in the bottom shelf of the linen cupboard if I wanted to fool the nurses.

One of my favorite places was out by the dumb-waiter. I learned to stretch as far as I could and lean over the edge of the dumb-waiter shaft. It was dark and you could smell food cooking and hear trays rattling in the kitchen downstairs. And I could talk to George. I'd call out, "George, are you there?" My voice sounded hollow. Then I would see his head with the tall white cap on it and he would boom out, "I got your favorite dish here today, Cardy." His voice sounded funny too.

I have no doubt that I frequently wandered off bounds. And I am certain that Gouldie and the nurses often felt like spanking me rather than reading me stories and giving me ice cream.

The times when I went outdoors, somebody always went with me. In the summer they used to take us riding in a big carriage drawn by horses. It had a bench on either side and was something like a paddy wagon, except that it was more open and the passengers were a lot younger than those who ordinarily travel under the supervision of the Police Department. We would go galloping down the streets to Central Park, and you could smell the horses and the grass and trees and see people in the shade having picnics.

One day Gouldie said, "Cardy, how would you like to go for a ride with me? Get your coat on."

"Where are we going?" I asked.

"You'll see" was all that she would tell me.

I reached up to clutch Gouldie's hand when we went down in the elevator. Outside we got into a real automobile. A man in a black uniform held the door open. Then he got in front and we drove away. The car went faster than anything

—faster than the horses that took us through the park. Pretty soon we came to a tall building and stopped.

"This is my house," Gouldie said, "and you are going to visit me."

The inside of Gouldie's house was like a house in a story book. The walls were blue, almost the color of the sky—not like the white walls in the hospital. There was furniture with red velvet cushions, and a china dog that sat in front of the fireplace. I thought it would be nice to live in a house with a fireplace and have a real dog, and I liked the little stool that Gouldie gave me to sit on.

"Wouldn't you like some tea?" Gouldie pulled a cord that was hanging on the wall, and a lady who had on a black dress and a little white apron came in with a silver tray. There was a big glass of milk for me and a silver teapot and a big plate of cookies. I could hardly eat, though, because I kept looking at the china dog.

Afterward Gouldie said, "Now I'm going to show you the garden."

The garden was the most wonderful place I had ever seen. It had a high, high fence and big bushes and a tree and paths that went everywhere. I went all over the garden and smelled the flowers and once I frightened a bird and it flew up onto the wall. It had rained that morning and I made a footprint with my boot in one of the flower beds.

"Look here, Cardy," Gouldie called.

Right in the middle of the garden there was a drain. Sticks and dirt had gotten caught there, and the rain made a wonderful pool. Gouldie looked up at the sky. "There's a nice breeze today—just right for sailing." She took a piece of paper out of her coat pocket. "Let's make some boats."

So Gouldie and I sailed boats in the garden, and I decided that was what I always wanted to do—sail boats and be with Gouldie. . . .

All the children in the ward were talking about it. Dr. Frauenthal was going to have a birthday, and we wanted to make a surprise for him. Finally we decided. One of the older girls made up a song, and I was the lucky one chosen to sing it. Families have a tendency to let their children show off, and the ward was my family. If a child can bleat like a goat, his relatives are doomed to listen to him perform until his voice changes.

It was a swell song—a parody on "Smiles"—something about "There are smiles for Miss Adams. There are smiles for Dr. Brown . . ." and the windup was: "But the biggest smile of all is for Dr. Frauenthal." I gave it everything I had. When I finished, my captive audience clapped loyally and those who had helped to write the song cheered.

Dr. Frauenthal said, "That was—" he cleared his throat— "that was very nice, children." And Gouldie, across the room, gave me a big smile. I felt almost as though it were my birthday too.

I had gradually gotten to know my mother as a nice lady who came to see me once in a while, and Gouldie liked her too. But I still was not prepared for the day that Mamma practically kidnaped me from the hospital.

She leaned over the table in the center of the ward where I was cutting paper strips to make a chain.

"You can come home now. You can play with your sisters, Terry and Lillian. Isn't that nice?" Her eyes were shining. "I brought a suitcase to pack your things."

Before I knew what was happening, we were standing by the Ward Supervisor's desk that had the white boxes above it she called "pigeonholes."

"Come back and visit us, Cardy," she said.

"I can't go until I say good-by to Gouldie," I complained.

"Gouldie isn't here today, but you'll see her again."

"But how will she find me?" I was crying. And I didn't believe her. I was sure I would never see Gouldie again.

My mother took me home on a streetcar. It was open on the sides and had high steps. She had to lift me up onto the straw seat, then she got in. I sat with my boots straight out in front of me but they did not reach the edge of the seat. Across the aisle a woman in an orange coat nudged the woman next to her and pointed at me. I held my mother's hand tight. Then I saw that everybody on the streetcar was looking. My mother put her arm around me and I hid my face next to her coat. I wanted to run away from all those people.

After we got off the streetcar my mother held my hand so high my feet hardly touched the ground. We had to walk a long way. When we got to the building that was her house there were some steps in front, but I was able to climb them. Then we went down a long hall and there was a stairway. I just looked at it. My legs hurt. My mother bent down toward me. "You are tired," she said, and she picked me up and carried me all the way to the top. When she set me down she was breathing hard. Her cheeks were rosy, and I decided that she was beautiful.

Then she unlocked a door and we went into a room.

She put me into a big stiff chair and said, "You rest now. I will be right back."

The house was darker than the hospital, and this room was smaller than the one at Gouldie's house.

Pretty soon Mamma came back with two girls in red dresses. They were both tall, lots taller than I, and they did not wear casts or braces.

"These are your sisters. This is Terry. This is Lillian." She smiled.

Terry and Lillian stood in front of the chair and looked at me. "Hello," they said shyly.

Mamma kept turning her head toward the door. Before long my father came in and she looked frightened.

"What's this—what are you doing here?" he said.

"Henry's home from the hospital." Mamma spoke as though she were trying hard to be happy. "The doctor signed the paper. He walks now—it's time he should be home, and I can take care of him."

My eyes filled with tears. What was I doing here? I did not know. I wanted to say, "I've had a good time visiting you, but I have to go back to the hospital now."

But I could not say a thing.

2

The World

The woods were dark. There were giants hiding behind the trees and fierce tigers crouched in the bushes.

I screamed. They were coming nearer. They would swallow me up.

I screamed louder.

There was a bright light and Mamma stood beside my bed. She hugged me close.

"It is all right. Nothing will hurt you," she soothed.

"It was dark," I cried. "The giants—"

"Everything will be all right now," Mamma said.

The woods were gone. I snuggled into her arms but could not stop sobbing.

"See, I'll leave a light in the hall, and you won't be afraid any more." She gently pulled the covers around me. Then she opened a picture book and read to me about the little hen who baked some bread.

I stopped sniffling to listen. It was warm and soft in my bed. I could hardly keep my eyes open. Mamma's voice was gentle and far away. . . .

Just before she left she kissed me on the cheek. . . .

There had always been a light in the hospital, even when we slept, as the night nurse worked over her charts at the desk and doctors made their regular rounds or came on an emergency call to visit a sick child. And Mamma kept a night light burning in our house from then on. At first, she did it for me. Then a few months later my sister Vicky was born, and by the time she was old enough not to require care at night, there was another baby in the family—Rose.

So the imaginary giants were banished. But I still had the real ones to contend with.

The children in our block—even those the same age as I— towered over me. When I smiled at them, they stared back. Some of them laughed. I was puzzled.

But it was not until I entered the first grade that I really understood.

Mamma and Papa had wisely chosen a flat in the same block as the school. It was on 101st Street near Amsterdam Avenue. My sister Terry took me to school the first day. Clutching her hand I hoisted myself up the steps to the school-yard. It was crowded with children, bouncing balls, playing hopscotch, and running up and down the steps. I had never seen so many children, not even at the hospital. And these were all so big. I tried to back away.

"What's the matter, Henry?" Terry patted my shoulder. "You'll be all right—soon as you get used to it."

Then I heard loud laughter. "Hey, Louie, looka the ape man."

Three big boys came toward me.

"I'll show you where your room is." Terry jerked my hand.

The laughs grew louder. "Come on, Henry," Terry urged. Her cheeks were red.

The crowd of jeering boys had grown. One of them, who had a thin face and dirty, light-colored hair, came over and shoved me. I shoved back, against his knee.

"Oh, you wanta fight, kid?"

"Cut it out, Mike," somebody yelled.

"You—you—leave my brother alone." Terry almost cried. But the circle of boys held us in.

"Hey, ape man, what you got tied to your feet, boxing gloves?"

I looked down at my mismatching boots. They weren't a bit like the shoes the other boys wore.

"I want to go home." I hung on Terry's arm, tears rolling down my cheeks.

"Sissy, sissy . . ."

Another big boy shoved me. I lost my balance and sprawled on the cement. Terry helped me up and brushed the dirt off my clothes. I started swinging my arms. The crowd pressed in and I couldn't see my sister anywhere.

Then the bell rang, and the boys ran into the building. Terry came back. "Here," she said, "blow your nose." She gave me her handkerchief. "Your hand's bleeding." I thought I saw tears in her eyes.

"Come on," she said. "I'll take you to your teacher."

The appellation of "ape man" was pretty accurate. With my dwarfed stature, my normally developed shoulders looked unusually broad, and my arms hung down almost to the ground.

Through the intervention of the teachers, the schoolyard hazing let up after the first day. (I found out later that all new children got their share.) My next encounter with the giants—the second and third graders—occurred off the school grounds.

It was a bright, clean day. School was over and I was coming from my room, reciting to myself something our teacher had read to us out of the first grade reader:

Dickie Dare went to school,
And on the way he met a cow.
"Moo, moo," said the cow. . . .

Since I was so slow in getting down the stairs, by the time
I reached the yard all the other children had gone. I liked
the schoolyard when it was empty. There was a tall fence
around it, with sharp spikes on top, and when I looked up at
the blue sky I could see towers on the building. They were
really turrets. I decided I was not in the schoolyard at all but
in a big castle. A cruel giant had made me a prisoner there,
but a brave knight was going to come in a minute and set me
free.

I reached the iron gate and took the big steps down to the
sidewalk—one, two, three . . .

"Hey, here comes the ape man—Hello, ape man."

I drew back toward the gate, but the four boys had surrounded me.

"Whatsa matter, shorty, cat got your tongue?"

A boy with a round fat face pulled my shirt out.

"You—leave me alone," I said weakly.

"Come on, ape man, let's take a walk." They pushed and
shoved me along the street.

Mike came up from behind. "You know what we were
talking about, Louie? Let's find out."

"Aw, leave the kid alone."

"Who ast you?"

"Pick on somebody your own size."

We came to a narrow space between two houses, and Mike
dived in, pulling me after him. The rest followed. I wanted
to fight back, but my arms were held by two of the gang
and my feet were no good for kicking. Where were they
going to take me? It was dark in here. I looked back toward
the street but a big boy blocked out the light. I looked ahead.

There was Mike. I felt myself shaking. Then we were in a yard in back of an empty store.

Mike leaned down and put his thin dirty face close to mine. His eyes glittered. He backed me up against a wall. I squirmed.

"Let me go!"

Another boy clapped a smelly hand over my mouth. "Stop yelling, kid, if you know what's good for you."

A third boy closed in. The one called Louie stood away from the others. "Let the kid go. You'll catch hell if his old lady hears this—"

"Shut up, Louie." The dirty face was close to mine. "We just wanta find out something, ape man. Take off your pants."

"No," I screamed, "No—No!"

The hand was clapped over my mouth and nose. I tried to bite but couldn't. I could hardly breathe.

"Ain't you ever been to the zoo?" another one sneered. "All apes look alike."

Rough hands tore at my pants and pulled them off.

There was silence.

"O.K., Mike, where's my nickel? He looks just like everybody else. Not cockeyed like you. I told ya—"

"Shut your face," Mike said.

They were gone.

Shaking and panting, my face hot, I put my clothes back on and limped home.

Fortunately the Mikes and the Louies soon tired of me, and eventually I was permitted to come and go without being noticed—that was as long as I stayed within the range of my own block. I was accepted as the crippled kid of our neighborhood, and gradually ignored by the swaggering bullies, which was all right with me.

The boys who were a lot older than I, however, began to

take a big-brotherly interest in me. I was a novelty and they competed for my attention.

One cold afternoon, the first fall I was home, three or four of them crouched around a small fire in the street by the curb.

The smoke smelled good and the fire was warm.

"Hi, kid," they said.

"Watcha doin'?" I asked.

"Roasting mickeys. Don't tell old Angelino. We snitched them from his place. Wanta sit down?"

Somebody plunged an open jackknife into the coals and stabbed a black potato. "Jeez but it's hot"—he dropped it.

The mickey was split open and hunks of the charred skin with its steamy insides passed around. It was the best potato I ever tasted, but it burned my tongue.

As I was wiping my mouth on the back of my hand, a long blue car went past. "Look at that buggy," one of them said. "It's got a chauffeur."

The car stopped and a lady got out. She looked up and down the street, and then she saw me and came over to the fire.

Why, it was Gouldie. I got up slowly and took her hand.

"Do you want to take me up to see your mother?" she said.

Walking down the street with Gouldie, with everybody looking at us, I felt as tall as anybody and very important. When we were away from the boys she stopped and took a good look at me.

"Cardy, you've grown. Your shoulders are broader and I think you have gained weight."

"You look just the same," I said. "You look pretty."

For a minute a rush of homesickness swept over me—for Gouldie and the hospital and the story books. But of course, I thought, you couldn't roast mickeys in the hospital.

"I'm glad you came," I said. "Mamma will be glad too. And I have a new baby sister."

Outside of our block, however, the jungle and the giants waited. The first time I remember venturing into this strange world was the day Mamma took me to the shoe store.

The boots which had been made for me while I was in the hospital, and the pairs that subsequently replaced them, were the most important physical item in my life. Although the boots, together with the small-size stockings Mamma bought and the elastic cuffs she put on my short trousers, certainly set me apart, they were still the rather crude bridge that brought me into the land of other children. They were prohibitively expensive. They had to be planned for, saved for, measured for, then painfully adjusted. And once they came into being they must be carefully nurtured through as long a life as possible.

New boots had to be ordered at an orthopedic shoe store on Fifty-third Street over on the east side. Since we lived on the west side, a trip to the shoe store was quite an expedition by streetcar and subway.

One Saturday morning, shortly before my seventh birthday, Mamma put on her good black dress, and I, scrubbed and polished and combed, donned my school suit and off we started to the shoe store.

"Take good care of Lillian and Victoria," Mamma said to Terry, who smiled a good-by to us from the door.

I liked walking down the street beside Mamma, even though she seemed awfully tall and far away. When we passed the laundry, the Chinese man smiled at us. And the lady in the candy store said hello. But once we had turned the corner at the end of our block I walked closer to Mamma and held on to her hand, even though after a while my arm ached from reaching up. I knew everybody was looking at us, so I kept my eyes straight ahead.

Suddenly I let go of my mother's hand. Running right toward me was a little white dog! I caught him in my arms. He licked my face and my hand, and tried to put his nose in my pocket.

"Mamma, Mamma, look at the dog. He has a piece of rope tied to his neck," I said. "Do you suppose he has run away?"

Just then a boy with red hair came running out of a store. At the boy's whistle the dog jerked his head and bounded toward him.

"Is that your dog?" I said.

"Yes," the boy answered. "Her name is Whitey. Do you want to pet her?"

That minute a woman carrying a lot of bundles came out of the store.

"Come here, Pat," she called. "Help me with this stuff— Who's that little crippled boy?"

Mamma reached down and took my hand, hard, and we almost flew through the streets. She didn't say anything to me, but her face was white and she was moving her lips as though she were whispering to herself.

After that the trip to the shoe store wasn't any fun. I kept wondering all day if Pat might have been my friend. And I wondered if I would ever see him again or get another chance to pet Whitey.

Why was I crippled? Maybe if I asked Mamma she would tell me. She knew almost everything—almost as much as Papa. Then a horrible thought came to me—supposing Mamma didn't know why? Maybe I had better not ask her.

I kept wondering about it, though.

The next Saturday morning I left the dining room where Vicky was creeping around the table and followed Mamma into the front room. She had a pitcher of water and was humming to herself. I decided I had to ask her, but I didn't know how.

Mamma looked up from watering the plants and smiled, so I guessed it was all right for me to stay. I never was allowed to play in this room. I didn't care very much because on the wall there was a picture of a man with bristly whiskers and he was scowling. Papa told me once that he was my great uncle who lived in Italy. He didn't seem very great to me, only cross.

Mamma had lots of plants. She grew herbs. When she made spaghetti sauce she would pick some sweet basil leaves and cook them with tomatoes and other things in the big kettle. The biggest plant of all was the one Mamma called a rubber plant. It didn't look like rubber really—just a plain plant with thick leaves. And it grew in a round brass dish with three legs. She was just pouring the rest of the water into the brass dish when I asked her, "Mamma, where were you born—in the hospital?"

"No," she said, "I was born in a house, in Italy." Then she added with a little twinkle, "In a small village just a stone's throw from Naples."

"Like Papa?"

"Yes, your father was born in Italy too, but we both came to New York when we were very small."

"I was born in a hospital though, wasn't I?"

"Yes, that is right."

"Well—" but I never got to the next question because there was a sharp rap at the hall door. Mamma jumped as though it frightened her. Then she went to the door.

It was Nona.

Nona was my grandmother. She had been born in Italy too and she lived upstairs. She bent down and put her hands on my shoulders. I looked at her beady eyes and the black hairs that grew on her upper lip, and turned to the side. She kissed me on the cheek. Her face felt dry and cold, not warm and soft like Mamma's.

"Anna," she said to my mother, "tell Onofrio to come upstairs right away when he comes from the barbershop. I have something important to say to him." She always called my father Onofrio because that was what she called him when he was her little boy in Italy, but his name was really Henry like mine.

"I—I guess I'd better go watch Vicky," I said, and raced clumsily out of the room.

Nona sent me to the store twice that day, and besides I played tag down in the street with the girls, so by the time I was ready for bed I was pretty tired.

"My legs hurt," I said to Mamma.

She drew her eyebrows together and pressed her lips into a line. "I know something that will take away the hurt."

She brought a big bowl of hot water and a towel and put them on a chair beside my bed. Then she bathed my legs till they were warm and tingly and patted them dry in the soft towel. Afterward, she rubbed them.

"That feels good," I said.

"Shall I read you *The Bobbsey Twins?*"

"All right," I said, "but—"

"Yes?"

"Mamma," I blurted out, "why are my legs different from other boys'?"

Mamma's beautiful face looked sad for a minute. "You were born like that," she said.

"But why? Why was I born that way?"

Mamma smiled a little. "Well," she said, "a lot of babies are born every year, and a certain number of them have to be crippled. I suppose God has to decide which ones. When you were born it must have been time for God to send

another crippled child into the world. So He looked around
at all the families. I think he decided that the Viscardis
would be a good family to have a little crippled boy."

Mamma's eyes looked shiny.

I thought for a minute. "Does God know how hard it is
for me to walk? And to go up the stairs?"

"Yes," Mamma said, "I'm sure He does. But He wants you
to be brave and have faith. That's why I say prayers to St.
Anthony, so that—so that maybe some day it won't be so
hard for you to walk."

Mamma did not tell me her part of the story then—nor
until many years later. From what I have learned, it must
have happened something like this:

In one of the wards at Sloane Maternity Hospital, nurses
were bringing in the babies for feeding. The lively bed-to-
bed conversations in Irish, Jewish, and Italian accents were
drowned out by the sudden shrill cries of a dozen or so hungry babies.

A nurse slid a practiced hand under one of the identical-
looking bundles and quickly brought it to my mother's bed.

"Here you are, Mrs. Viscardi."

My mother smiled, feeling tired but content. Her baby
was only a day old but he had a good strong cry. She looked
at his contorted face and the moist black hair covering his
pink head. She was especially lucky—her baby was a boy. A
girl at home and now a boy. What a big christening party
they would have for the first-born boy!

While the babies were being fed, the woman in the next
bed looked across at my mother and frowned.

"My baby's feet are cold."

Without disturbing the baby she was nursing, my mother
slid her hand gently under the blanket to see if his feet were
cold.

But the baby's feet were not there.

She felt sick. Quickly her hand darted to the bell to summon the nurse. In tears she demanded, "What's the matter with my baby?"

The nurse carefully replaced the baby's blanket. "He was born that way," she said, "but you must not worry. The doctor will do everything he can . . ."

Later, when my father stopped by the bed with a little bouquet of flowers, my mother told him. "There's something wrong with the baby."

The next day a doctor came in to talk to her. "Why was my baby born like that?" she asked.

"No one knows. But don't worry—he'll be all right."

In the weeks that followed it became apparent to her that her baby would not be all right. And my mother kept torturing herself by asking: Why did it happen? Was it my fault? She could see that my father was worried too.

Some of the relatives said it was because of the time she was so frightened back in the second or third month up at Nona's. It was one of the days that Nona went into a trance. Each member of the family was permitted to enter the dark room and ask her a question. My mother still trembled when she remembered it months later. She had not wanted to go in when her turn came. When she entered the room, Nona started chanting strange words. My mother began to shiver. She ran out of the room. The others told her she was deathly white.

They said a fright could mark a baby, but the doctors said no.

The day of the christening, although my mother cooked a fine dinner and had *cannoli* and cream puffs, and although my father looked jaunty and proud when he carried me home from the church in the family christening robe, it was a quiet occasion—just the relatives. Nona in black with her shawl pulled over her bony shoulders, the whiskery uncles, and the aunts—the vinegary one and the pretty ones. My father had bought several bottles of wine, but there was no singing, and everybody went home early.

The christenings of his children were among the occasions when Papa went to church. Like many men of his social group, he followed the easy Old World customs. A feast day was important because you did not work that day. Church was for women: men had other things to do. I always thought of Papa and his Italian friends when I listened to the church-yard scene in *Cavalleria Rusticana*. As the church bells ring, the women cover their heads and go in. The men stay out-side and sing.

One Sunday, a few weeks after I had passed from the first to the second grade, Papa decided to take me to Mass. I was so anxious to go that I combed my hair myself and slicked it down with water and got my fingernails good and clean. Papa had on a bright blue suit and a polka-dotted tie. Mamma beamed with approval as we set forth.

But as we stopped by the holy-water font a man at the church door looked at me sharply and whispered something to Papa. The other people stared at us too.

What is wrong? I wondered. Do you suppose crippled children are not allowed to come to church any more?

Papa took my hand and led me outside. "Let us go for a walk in the park," he said, smiling brightly.

My eyes were smarting. "What's the matter, Papa?" I finally said. "Why didn't we stay for Mass? Is it because I'm crippled?" I could hardly get the words out.

Then Papa threw back his head and laughed. And he laughed again.

"Oh, this is very funny," he said.

I did not think it was funny, and I wished I had never come to church with him. I had a salty taste in my mouth.

Then he put both his hands on my shoulders and looked right into my eyes. "Oh, this is very funny—no children allowed at eleven o'clock Mass. What a way to run a church!"

I laughed too, just to be polite.

"We men will have to go to the poolroom," Papa said. Then he laughed again. "Come, Henry, we will go to Central Park. You like that?"

Central Park. That was a place outside of our block. But with Papa it would be all right to go. Nobody would call me names or chase me. They'd better not.

Papa whistled a little tune. "It's from an opera," he told me. And he swung my arm as we went along the streets. In the park everything was nice and green. It reminded me of the time when I was in the hospital and used to go to the park. Papa took me on a path across a bridge. There was water down below and people were rowing boats. Then he took me to a bench and we bought some peanuts from a man and fed them to the pigeons. He bought me a balloon too— a big purple one.

"You must have gone to High Mass," Mamma said when we came in. "You were away two hours."

Although Papa did not take time to go to church regularly, and Mamma never seemed to have the time, what with cooking and scrubbing and mending, they arranged for us children, as we were growing up, to attend Sunday School at our parish church which was just a few blocks away. Also, I was excused from school early, one day a week, to receive religious instruction. Eventually I took my first Communion.

When Papa came home from his barbershop downtown, he had many things to do. Nona, between pinches of snuff and the casting of spells, was always sending for him to mend a chair or fix a faucet up at her flat. The rest of the time he experimented in our kitchen with the shaving cream he was inventing, or sat at the golden oak dining-room table planning ways to make a killing in Wall Street on the tips furnished by his patrons, so that he could retire to a life of ease.

I never knew whether to talk to him or not. Sometimes he would swing me up in the air, high, and set me on top of the bookcase. He would sing words I did not understand though they sounded good, and he would grin and swing me down to the floor again, where I would stand and look up at him. Days like that I thought he was very handsome. But there were other days, especially after he had been up at Nona's place, when he would be gruff and say, "Go away and don't bother me."

For a child growing up in a neighborhood such as ours, the social center was the street. The street was where the fire engines clanged past, led by their galloping black horses; where the ice wagon stood on hot days and you could hook ice while the man was making a delivery; where the police patrol careened around the corner on two wheels en route to the scene of a crime; where neighborhood loyalties were sealed and feuds deepened by lusty dramatic acts; and where important athletic contests took place.

When I had become more or less used to this turbulent world, I began to venture into the street after school and on Saturdays.

The storekeepers permitted me to come inside when it rained and the Chinese laundryman used to let me watch him slide his heavy iron back and forth on the board. It was partly due, I am sure, to the fact that Mamma drilled me in etiquette daily. In our block a child who said, "No, thank you, I don't care for any," or "Will you please tell me what time it is?" was a sensation. Also I think the tradespeople decided I was harmless. Even if I should take it into my head to pilfer a few lollipops or a bunch of pennies from the till, I could be caught red-handed with the loot before I reached the door. So I enjoyed a sort of diplomatic immunity not usually granted to normal seven-year-olds.

The other children, by the way, were gradually accepting me in their games—at least as an onlooker. At first I bounced a ball with Terry and Lillian and their friends, or swung a rope for them to jump over. But as I grew more venturesome I gradually wandered down to the other end of the block where a lively game of Kick the Stick was usually in progress. It was a tenement version of baseball—in which a rough sort of diamond was laid out in the street, and a stick kicked from base to base. Although I could not play this game, after watching it for a season I became expert at the finer interpretations of the rules. I could call out "Foul"—"You're out" —or "He's safe" with a ring of authority. Unfortunately my decisions were not always accepted, and sometimes I was chased off the "field" by an angry team.

The game I liked best was marbles. The first time, I watched from the curb while a crowd of older boys were shooting immies across a manhole cover. When the game was over a boy with a big bag of them said to me, "Come on out, kid." He made room for me beside him, and from then on that was my regular place.

One day, when the game broke up, old "Marble Bags" had made an unusually good haul and was practicing some tricky shots. I watched. "You're good," I said.

"Say, kid, would *you* like to try?"

I took the shooter he handed me, and he set up three marbles on the manhole cover. "All right, try to hit those. No—not that way, curve your fingers some more. . . . That's right. Now— Nice shot for a beginner!"

If he had given me a big chocolate soda I could not have been any happier. I had made a good shot!

In the years that followed, under the tutelage of Marble Bags I gradually became the immies champ of our block, and my self-esteem grew along with my big bag of marbles. In later years I was often to think with pride of that little achievement, as I watched amputees and paraplegics regain a feeling of personal dignity through mastering the art of doing something well with their hands.

The street was also a place where lessons were learned.

One hot day in the summer it was quiet in our block. Across the street a boy named Buster sat alone on the curb because his mother would not let him go swimming with the other big boys. Buster was his nickname because he had a Buster Brown haircut with bangs. It looked funny. I had my hair cut like the other boys. In the summer Papa clipped it real close to my head and he kept it trimmed with a pair of barber shears that hung on a nail in the kitchen.

That morning I had found a rubber ball, so I went down the street to Denny's house. "Wanta play ball?" I called down the basement stairs.

Denny looked through the bars on the window. "O.K.," he said. "My old man's drunk, but I don't think he'll wake up. Ma's away."

Denny was going into the third grade just as I was, but the other boys in our room didn't like to play with him because he smelled funny. I had gotten used to the smell. It was not so bad if you didn't get close to him, and he was a pretty good ballplayer. Mamma always said, "It's too bad nobody looks after that boy."

Denny got on one side of our steps and I got on the other and we threw the ball across. Then we tried fancy shots like hitting the door frame to make the ball bounce onto the sidewalk. Once after I had thrown it real hard it hit the fire escape and flew off and landed out in the street, way over near the other side.

Buster ran out to get it. Just then an automobile came by. The driver pulled the emergency brake and stopped right

in front of Buster. He swore so loud I bet you could hear
him in Central Park. Buster gave him a smarty smile and
threw the ball over. "Lousy shot," he said, and then slouched
into his house. The man drove off, still swearing.

"Don't be so smart, Henry, you almost hit Lil!" Terry
shrieked. She was on the stoop reading a book to Lil and
Vicky, but Vicky was not listening. She was pulling herself
down the steps one by one, and then back up again. Her
white bloomers were almost black where she sat.

Over by Buster's house a woman had stopped to talk to
the garbage man. He pointed our way, and as she started
across the street I saw that she was a Negro, but she had a
large white mark on her face.

"Terry—look!" I called.

"She's coming over here to get us," Denny said. "Run!"

Terry scooped up Vicky and rushed down. Lil clanged the
gate and we all crouched by the basement door. I didn't like
being so close to Denny but there wasn't much I could do
about it.

The woman was going up our steps.

We waited. Then she came down and looked around the
corner at us. Lil screamed.

The woman looked surprised and a little bit sad, then she
went on down the street.

When we told Mamma, her face was serious. "Terry," she
said, "you are a big girl. You should know better. And Henry
too. It is wrong to think that people are bad just because
they are different. I am ashamed of you children. And it is
cruel to laugh."

After the girls had gone into the bedroom, Mamma turned
to me. "Henry, you especially should know how it feels to
have people stare at you. That woman has feelings too—the
same as you. Remember that."

I stared down at the worn linoleum under my bunchy

boots. Mamma was unhappy, and I was sorry. But I didn't tell her so.

One of the nicest things about summertimes had been the carrousel. It was on a big platform with heavy iron wheels, and a man sat up in front and drove the horses that pulled it along the street. It always stopped by Buster's house. Then the man turned a handle and the carrousel started to go around. Another man made music by cranking a hurdy-gurdy. If you paid a penny you could ride—on a horse or a duck or a swan.

When the men got ready to take the carrousel away, the driver would say "Giddap" to the horses and they would start off. Buster used to jump and catch on the side of the platform so he could get a free ride down the block. But one day he didn't quite make it. I was in front of our house and saw it happen—he fell into the street. I did not want to look but I couldn't turn away. The iron wheels rolled right over his legs. Buster screamed so loud that Mamma opened a window in our front room and said, "Are you children all right? Don't leave the house!" And Nona stuck her head out of her window and yelled, "Who's screeching down there?"

The kids across the street shouted to the man to stop. He jumped down to look at Buster lying there. I felt sick at the noises Buster made. Then everybody crowded around and I couldn't see him any more.

Mamma was on the stoop by now. "You see how dangerous it is to play in the street," she said.

We watched silently as the men carried Buster into the house. He was still screaming. After a while a policeman came and talked to the men; and then an ambulance came, and they took Buster away on a stretcher. He was quiet then. The carrousel stayed there for a long time, but nobody rode on it.

There was no playing in the street the next day. Nor the next.

The woman in the candy store told my mother that Buster's legs were crushed and they would have to be cut off.

Buster will be crippled like me, I thought, besides having that terrible haircut. I was sorry.

That was the first and certainly the most vivid demonstration I ever had of how quickly a healthy child, or adult for that matter, can become crippled. That one moment with the horrible thump of the wheels going over Buster's legs would make the difference.

But Buster did not become a crippled boy. A week later news traveled through the block that he had "blood poisoning." The next day he died.

Marble Bags and two other boys came past our house one morning.

"Do you wanta see Buster?" they said. "They brought him home last night."

I did not know whether I wanted to see Buster or not. "Sure, I guess so," I said. I decided not to ask Mamma.

Buster's flat was full of people. His mother sat in the front room with a handkerchief up to her eyes, and a lot of neighbors were around her talking in low voices.

There was a casket across one corner. It was smaller than the casket they took Mr. Goldberg to the cemetery in. He was a man down the street who had died.

I was glad that Buster's casket was up so high that I could not see him; but when we got close to it, before I knew what was happening, one of the big boys lifted me up, and I looked. Buster had on his good suit and his eyes were closed, but his face was awfully thin and it looked cold like the statue of St. John in church. I think he had rouge on. His haircut did not seem funny any more.

"Put me down, put me down," I said. I wanted to run away, but in the room full of tall people I could hardly move. I thought I was going to die because I could not breathe. Pushing and squeezing, I hobbled painfully to the door. Outside I took deep breaths of the fresh air.

Anyway, I thought, Buster won't have to be crippled.

For a long time after that I was worried. Suppose that I should die? Or Mamma? Or one of the girls? Or Papa? Or Nona? Nona was old but it did not seem as though she would ever die.

Mostly I thought about dying myself. I stopped playing in the street, and I always was careful when I crossed, especially so when it rained, or in the winter when it was icy. If I should ever trip—what happened to Buster might happen to me.

Then it was summer again and all the boys went swimming every day—even Denny.

What could I do? The water would ruin my boots. Yet, if I took them off I would not be able to stand up, and I knew I could not swim.

But one day some of the big boys came by and called up to ask Mamma if I could go for a walk—over by the river. Mamma finally said yes, but be careful.

I walked part of the way, and when I got tired they hoisted me up on their shoulders. Then I really was tall—taller than seven feet. We came to the railroad tracks. I had never been this far from home except with Mamma or Papa, and it was exciting.

"Look at that old cardboard," Marble Bags said. It was a big piece. It must have been wrapped around a mattress or something.

"Let's build a shelter."

An empty freight car stood on a track and the boys put

the cardboard under it and bent it like the sides of a house. Then we all crawled inside and they talked about baseball and girls. It started to rain, so we stayed. It was just like being in a clubhouse. One of the boys took out a cigarette butt and lit it.

"Give me a puff," somebody said.

"Look, the sun's out. Let's go swimming." Marble Bags ran across the tracks and down to the river where he peeled off his pants and shirt and dived off a big rock.

The other boys picked me up, and we ran after him.

I sat on the bank and watched them paddle around.

"Come on in," they yelled. "We'll hold you up."

Did I dare? Of course, they said. Hesitantly I took off all my clothes except my boots, and two of them let me down over the side of the rock.

"It's cold," I shrieked. But as soon as I had been in the water a minute it felt wonderful. I paddled with my short legs while they held onto my hands.

"I can swim! I can swim—almost," I gasped.

When we got home, Mamma said, "You were caught in the rain. Your hair is wet . . . Your shoes are wet too."

I smiled secretly.

But there were many afternoons when I was not taken along by the gang. As a result I spent a lot of time in the house.

We had a cat that was wild. He would jump at you from the top of a cupboard or out of a dark corner. One day I decided: I'll fix this cat. So, making believe I was going to give him some milk or something, I went up to him slowly. When he came toward me, I grabbed his fur. He squirmed, but I took a piece of cord out of my pocket and tied him up. He wriggled and scratched but he was soon trussed up tighter than a strait jacket. Then I slipped the other end of the cord through the bar on the back of the Morris chair. I tugged and pulled, and soon pussy was swinging back and forth just out of reach of the floor. He was all hunched up and tried to spit at me. I tied the cord and sat there watching him. Mamma heard me laughing and hurried in from the kitchen where she was giving Rose a bath. Rose was just a month old.

Mamma's face was a picture of sorrow, but her eyes blazed. "Henry, how can you be so cruel! That cat—it's suffering. Let it free at once." I thumped out to the kitchen, stretched up to reach Papa's barber shears, and came back and cut the cord. Kitty shook himself a couple of times and the rope slipped off. He scooted under the bed in the next room.

When Mamma had put Rose in bed for her nap, she came out to the dining room where I sat winding up the cord and unwinding it. She was very quiet and her face looked severe.

"I am going to punish you for what you did to the cat," she said. "We have five children now and you act more like the baby than Rose does."

Mamma was calmer than I had ever seen her before. I wondered what she was going to do.

"A boy nine years old is too big to spank, but you are going to be spanked."

The spanking did not hurt, really. What was worst was that Mamma did not speak to me the rest of the day.

And when the cat would see me coming he would glide under the couch and his yellow eyes would glare at me out of the dark. I never teased the cat again.

That same Morris chair was my favorite reading place. To get into it I had to put my hands up on one arm and then hoist myself up and flip around into the seat, the way a swimmer pulls himself up onto a dock from the water. I read all the books we had in the house and all that I could borrow from the school library. Papa had strong feelings about books not bound in cloth: no paper-backed books were permitted in our house. That still gave me considerable latitude, though, for my literary pursuits. From Dickie Dare and the Little Red Hen I advanced to Tom Swift, the Rover Boys, and eventually wound up somewhere between *Twenty Thousand Leagues under the Sea* and Albert Payson Terhune.

In Papa's strivings for culture he also bought me a violin for Christmas one year. Disgusted that it was not a sled, I refused to have anything to do with it. Papa never pressed the issue of my taking music lessons, although Terry did practice on the piano a lot. She played a song called "Over the Waves," till the whole family got seasick. And Mamma, when coaxed, would play her battered old mandolin. We teased her because her favorite song was "Rosie O'Grady," but I really thought she sang quite well.

Papa's code called for giving his children a special treat on Sundays. Mamma always had us dressed and ready early in the day for our jaunt. To Central Park, to the Aquarium, to the Statue of Liberty—somewhere different every week. I never worried about anybody making fun of me when I was with Papa. He looked handsome in his Homburg hat and he stared back at people in a jaunty way. When we reached home Papa's relatives descended on the house in a garlicky parade and ate with gusto and incessant chatter the good dinner Mamma had spent the day preparing.

One especially nice Sunday, Papa took the girls and me out to Queens on the subway. When we got off the train we walked to a field of yellow daisies just back of the station.

"I'm going to pick a big bouquet for Mamma," I said, "enough to fill the brass bowl the rubber plant used to grow in." And I started into the field. The daisies were almost up to my shoulders and they were tossing their black eyes in the breeze.

"A fine idea," Papa said. "Let's pick bouquets. It's just like a field of gold." He stood there dreamily looking at the expanse of flowers. "Just like gold, hey?" His eyes sparkled as he threw back his head and laughed.

Though the years were to bring separation and death, and I never would really understand Papa, I felt then as though I knew him. I wanted to stay there all day with him and the girls, in the field under the warm sun. But I knew that eventually we would have to go back to the loud laughter and the spontaneous belching and, worst of all, the interminable Italian conversation of the relatives; and I would have to watch Mamma, Madonnalike and patiently smiling even though she was not having any fun.

Another Sunday we went fishing, Papa and I and Terry. It was the summer I was ten years old. Papa took us to a place called City Island where we rented a rowboat. They fished, but I lay back in the boat, rocking up and down with the waves, and it seemed as though I were all alone on the water watching the sea gulls soaring overhead. When Papa got tired of fishing he rowed ashore, and he carried me above the high-water mark to the beach, where we ate the sandwiches Mamma had packed and drank coffee from Papa's thermos bottle. Then Papa took a nap and Terry and I threw stones into the water and played Duck on the Rock.

Some weeks later Mamma said to me, "How would you like to move to the country? To Long Island."

Remembering that Sunday, I answered, "When? Can we go right away?"

Mamma's eyes glowed. "We are going very soon. We have bought a house—"

"A whole house like this?"

"No, an attached house. For just one family."

"How wonderful! Can I have a dog? Will there be a boat?"

We were going to live near the water. A whole new life spread out before me.

"And a whole house just for ourselves!"

"Well," Mamma explained, "your grandmother and your uncles and aunts have helped pay for the house. They will live in the upstairs and we will live downstairs."

Part of the beautiful dream melted, like *spumone*.

But still—I could hardly wait.

3

Another World

The woods on Long Island were cool and shady. They came up almost to our back porch. I could be alone in the woods. I could find out where violets grew in the spring. I could go exploring. I could be Jim Hawkins on Treasure Island, or Sir Lancelot on the way to meet Lady Guinevere. On a sunny day I could relive "The Goldbug," and when it rained I could paddle rafts across the pools where the water stood. It was like country I had read about in books. And it made me realize how much I had disliked the smothering life and the staring crowds of the city.

The school did not have an iron-spiked fence around it. It was just a wooden building two stories high with a fire escape and outside toilets. The principal, a tall, gray-haired woman, stood on the front steps every morning and rang a hand bell.

Mamma went with me the first day to register; I was going into the fifth grade. As I peered up at the principal across the top of her desk, I decided she was kind. She reminded me of Gouldie a little. I smiled. Then she said, "We will take good care of your boy."

I felt my hair growing bristly in back.

"Instead of coming up with the other pupils he will enter and leave school by the fire escape. That will be easier."

What was she talking about? Why should I come up the outside stairway all alone just because I couldn't walk as fast as the others?

"I am very strong," I said, "and I have good grades from my other school."

Her pitying smile shut me out. "I am interested in your welfare. It is my duty to see that you are protected at all times. I am my brother's keeper."

This "brother's keeper" attitude, though it may spring from the kindliest of motives, is one of the biggest obstacles a disabled person must overcome in his battle to live as a human being. Many times since that day I have thought of that unfortunate woman who so earnestly desired to help me. At the time, though, my attitude toward her was perhaps less charitable.

Dutifully I climbed the fire escape every day. She thinks I can't do as well as the other kids, I thought. All right, I'll show her. So I dallied along the way to school, talking to the postman and the neighbors, with the result that I usually arrived a few minutes after the bell had been rung and the other pupils were safely inside. Then I would start climbing. Every third or fourth step I would stop and turn around to take a breath of the clean air and look down at the school-yard and Mrs. Baker's chickens over in the next block. By the time I reached my room, the other pupils were settled at their desks and the teacher had started the geography lesson. Then I would open the door wide, letting in a draft of cold air, smile innocently and limp to my seat, where I slammed down my books and pencils with as much clatter as possible.

It worked. As the days became colder, the teacher's starts at my sudden entrances became more violent and were usually accompanied by titters from the girls and horsy snickers from the boys. One bitter cold day a gust of wind yanked the door out of my hand. It banged against the side of the building, and a pile of arithmetic papers blew off the teacher's desk and settled all over the room.

The next day I was told that to avoid confusion in the classroom I would "hereafter come and go with the others."

Although our neighborhood was open country by contrast to 101st Street, we really lived in a town—Elmhurst. To get to our house you rode out from Manhattan on the subway to the next to the last stop. Then you walked quite a way until you came practically to the end of a street—it wasn't even paved—and there we were. I had been curious from the start about what an "attached house" was. When I saw ours it reminded me of Siamese twins I had seen on a circus poster— it seemed to be grown to the house next door on one side. It was a real house, though, with an upstairs and a downstairs and a big stoop, except that now we called it a porch. I did not go upstairs unless I had to, because that was where Nona and my uncles and aunts and cousins lived. The basement was fascinating though.

That was where Papa and Uncle Nick had their workshop. Uncle Nick was an inventor, and they had all sorts of saws and hammers, and a workbench with a vise and different-sized nails. I used to sneak down when they were there, in hopes that I would find them working on an invention, but mostly they would just be sitting talking about the stock they had bought in Parker Axles that was going to make them rich very soon.

I finally decided that Uncle Nick was better at getting ideas than at making something. Papa was no carpenter but he was handy at repairs. One thing he did was to get me a tricycle and put crude wooden blocks on the pedals so that I could use it.

The following year I got a wagon, which had belonged to my cousins upstairs but was not the right size for any of them. It was fine for me. I would put my right leg in the wagon, the leg that I could bend, and I would push with the other one. Now I could go anywhere. Before, I always had to stop when my legs got tired from pedaling.

Another advantage of the wagon was that when I was coasting around in it people did not stare at me; I must have looked like anyone else. Elmhurst was less crowded than our neighborhood in New York too, and perhaps that made a difference.

One afternoon when I was out coasting it started to rain. I had a long way to go, and the rain came down hard before I got close to home. It was cold and I wished I had worn my sweater. On the way, passing a vacant lot, I heard a whimpering noise. I stopped, and out from under a bush came a small brown dog. He was soaking wet and shivering and he didn't have a collar on.

He put his paws up on the edge of the wagon and whined. I'll take him along, and maybe find out where he lives, I thought. So I hoisted him into the wagon and he crawled under my arm. I could feel him shaking against me.

When I got home he was still with me. I made him stay on the porch while I let myself into the kitchen quietly.

Mamma was at the table kneading dough. I leaned on the seat of a chair and took off my cap. A stream of water ran down the side of my face.

Mamma looked at me. "It must be raining hard."

I nodded. "What are you doing?"

Without slowing down her easy movements, she answered, "Making noodles for *lasagna*."

I watched her floury fingers move over the board.

"Mamma," I said, "there's a lost dog outside. He came home with me. Can I bring him in?"

She smiled. "Did he follow you home or did you bring him? All right. He can come."

But just then Papa came bursting through the back door, shaking rain off his big umbrella.

"Where did that dirty pup come from?" He looked at me. "Get him off our property."

"But, Papa, he's wet and cold and he's lost. Can't I just bring him in and get him warm?"

Papa stomped into the front hall, muttering, "Why must you have a dog?" Mamma smiled and went to work cutting the noodles.

I brought the dog inside. His coat was all matted. Mamma wrinkled her nose. "That dog needs a bath."

Vicky came in from the dining room with her doll.

"Hello, doggie," she said. The puppy licked her hand. "Is he ours?" Her eyes were shining. This made me feel good because Vicky usually looked sad and pale.

After supper Lil and I gave him a bath in Mamma's wash-tub. He only got away from us twice, though one time he ran into the front room and shook water all over Papa's newspaper, and Papa was mad. When the dog was dry his hair was reddish brown and soft, so I named him Jerry after "Jerry of the Islands." He slept under the stove that night.

The next day I took Jerry all over town in the wagon, but we couldn't find out where he lived, so I had to keep him.

Sometimes Jerry rode in the wagon, but when he grew older and stronger he ran along behind. When winter came I had a sled, and he would chase me on the sled.

One day I was coasting down a hill near the school when I took a curve too fast. The sled jerked sideways and I fell off with my leg doubled under me. I pulled myself up on my hands and brushed the snow off my pants, but when I tried to stand up a sharp pain shot through my leg. My foot slipped on the ice and I crumpled to the ground. Jerry came up barking impatiently.

What was I going to do? There was no one around. It was getting dark and a cold wind was blowing. I tried again, but I could not put any weight on my right leg. My sled was way down at the bottom of the hill. So I just sat and let myself slide down toward it. Jerry followed, nipping at my sleeves and nudging me with his nose. I guess he thought it was a new game. When we reached the sled I climbed on and started pushing with my "good" leg.

It was pitch dark when I got home. The kitchen light was on and Mamma was on the back porch looking out toward the woods and calling. Her dress was blowing around her.

"Where have you been?" she said. "I was worried."

I told her about my leg.

"Oh, you're hurt! Put your arm around me and I'll help you up the steps."

That night Papa took me back to the hospital in a taxicab. If my leg had not throbbed so much I might have enjoyed the ride. The hospital was not the same. Gouldie was gone, but Dr. Frauenthal was still there. I stayed a week and they took X-rays and put my leg in splints. I remember it hurt.

But even though my leg was stiff and sore, I was certainly glad that I could get hurt like other boys riding on a sled.

In the other half of our house was a family of boys, the Bakers. They were all grown up except Raymond, who was about my age, and Walter, who was younger. Raymond had had "infantile paralysis" and, ever since, his legs had been just like rubber. He could not stand on them. He either walked on crutches or dragged himself along on his hands, like a seal.

There was one peculiar thing about Raymond—he played

the violin. He really didn't play it, he only practiced on it. And Nona said it sounded just like cart-wheel squeaks. For once I agreed with Nona. I think the only reason Raymond kept sawing away at his fiddle was because his mother used to yell at him that if he didn't practice she would beat his brains out. I guess she really didn't mean it, though.

Raymond's family were always having fun and they did a lot of singing and laughing, especially on Saturday nights.

I liked Raymond because nothing seemed to bother him and because he was so strong. He could saw down trees and chop wood. Sometimes he and I would go out to the woods to look for his mother's chickens. She didn't keep them fenced in and they were always going to roost in the bushes.

One morning I was out on the back porch waiting for Mamma to get breakfast when I heard a loud cackling coming from Raymond's house. Then I heard his mother shouting. In a minute the screen door opened and out stalked a young hen with her head high, and right behind her came Raymond's mother looking almost as proud. She was carrying an egg.

"Look, Henry, her first egg. She laid it under the kitchen table. I want for Vicky to have it. Maybe it will help her appetite."

I looked up at her round, plump face and took the warm egg she handed me over the railing that separated their end of the porch from ours. She gave my hand a squeeze. Raymond's mother was pretty nice.

But as the months passed it became apparent that it would take more than the kindly interest of neighbors and a nourishing diet to bring back Vicky's health. She just had not gotten the good start the other girls had.

We had lived in Elmhurst for three years. Terry was fifteen and in high school and very grown up. I was thirteen and ready for my last year in grammar school, but I still used my coaster wagon because it was easier for me to get around that way. Lil was eleven and quite pretty, and Vicky was seven. But she was so thin and frail that it seemed as though Rose, who was only four, might decide to shoot up ahead of her any year now.

Except for my trips to the hospital, doctors were practically unheard of in our family. Papa did not believe in doctors and the only one he ever consulted was a homeopath who used to give him pills that were all different colors, but always the same size.

So I was quite surprised one Saturday when Mamma told me, "I am going to take Vicky to see the new doctor this afternoon. Your father does not know about it. He might not like it. Do you want to come?"

"Sure," I said. "I'll give Vicky a ride in my wagon."

The new doctor was a young man who had opened offices on the first floor of a white house just a few blocks from where we lived. After I had proudly escorted my two ladies there, I sat outside in the wagon while Jerry scampered back and forth across the lawns, smelling of bushes and trees and acting important.

It seemed to take them hours. Finally a big man came out. He looked like a football player. He had dark hair and his eyes twinkled.

"Hello," he said. His voice was friendly. "Your mother and Vicky will be out in a few minutes."

"Are you the doctor?"

"Yes, I'm Dr. Yanover, and I understand your name is Henry."

I stood up. "I hope my sister is going to be all right."

"Don't worry about her. We're going to make her well." He sat down on the steps and took a pipe out of his pocket. While he was lighting it, he looked at me sharply. "How are *you?*"

"Fine."

"That's some wagon you've got. Easy to get around in?"

"Sure. I can go everywhere."

"How about those boots? Are they comfortable?"

"Oh, yes, sir." But I guess I did not sound very convincing.

"Do your legs get tired when you walk a lot?"

"Yes."

"Do they give you pain sometimes?"

"Well—yes."

I did not usually talk to strangers that way, but this man didn't seem like a stranger. Jerry certainly liked him. He put his paws on Dr. Yanover's knee and licked his suit.

"Here come your mother and Vicky now." Dr. Yanover got up and patted Jerry's head. He bowed to Mamma. "Good-by, Vicky. I'll see you again, Hank."

I felt shy, yet I wanted to say something. "Thank you. It was nice talking to you."

That was how Dr. Yanover became our Unofficial Family Doctor, and from that time on he made occasional visits to our house. He soon had Vicky's illness, a kidney ailment, under control. And he kept a watchful eye on the rest of us while we were growing up.

It was many years later that I learned how Dr. Yanover, after finishing his final internship in surgery at City Hospital in New York, had loaded his books and a few other possessions into a patient's wagon and come across the bridge to Queens to start a practice. Unrebuffed by the advice of a local druggist to "Go back to Manhattan—we don't like your kind here," he had engaged rooms with a friendly Irish family whose loyalties were not confined to their own religious group, in return for his promise to look after the health of their four children and make what financial reimbursement he could. The professional skill of this warmhearted man gradually became known throughout our section of the city.

Today he is the chief surgeon of a private hospital there and enjoys the highest reputation in medical circles.

Not long after he came to Elmhurst, Dr. Yanover's keen eyes lighted on me. He wondered who I was, and whether I was getting good care. The day that Mamma took Vicky to see him, he said to Mamma, "Do you happen to know the boy outside with the wagon?" She told him that I was her son.

Although two world wars have caused a progressive approach to physical medicine and rehabilitation programs, it is unfortunate for the crippled child growing up and the incapacitated veteran returning home that there are still too few people with Dr. Yanover's attitude. He did not try to ignore my disability, nor did he give me pity. He accepted it as a fact and me as a person.

One of my saddest experiences with a thoughtless individual came at a crucial period during adolescence—my graduation from grammar school.

This was to be a big occasion. The little wooden schoolhouse had been replaced by a modern fireproof building— all brick and glass. We loved it and our class was to be the first one graduated from the new school. The new principal planned to put on a bang-up graduation exercise as a climax to his first year. Program, music, speeches—all were carefully planned. I had developed an interest in public speaking, so I was one of the happiest kids in the class when I was chosen to recite Lincoln's Gettysburg Address. I had a new suit for the occasion, and Mamma had taken special pains with her customary alterations. We always bought boys' suits with short pants, and then she cut off the trousers halfway up and pleated them into an elastic cuff that fitted above the top of my boots.

In arranging the processional the principal had thirty students to get down the side aisles and up onto the stage. Obviously a dwarfed, crippled boy in the middle of one line would slow things up and make it uncomfortable for himself and everyone else. The principal finally decided on a way to eliminate embarrassment, for everyone but me. He put me at the end of the line.

So, the day of my first graduation—and no subsequent graduation is ever quite so important—I thumped in at a long interval after my classmates, and arrived at the platform hot and flustered, almost panting, when it could have been arranged for me to enter unobtrusively from the wings. This time the side door would have been the right way. When I rose for my part on the program I was sure that everyone in the auditorium felt sorry for me, and I am afraid that my halfhearted rendition of the Address from my well of self-pity was a sad tribute to a great man.

One of the things about the new school that we boys liked best was the gymnasium. I found one game at which I could hold my own: that was handball, which was not really so different from the game I had played with Denny in front of the house on 101 Street. I was best at doubles. By using a tricky serve and "killer" placement shots, I could handle the in-court, with a partner who could range the back court and cover the greater height and distance required. At times like this I could forget my limitations. It was swell fun.

During the summer vacation after we graduated from grammar school, an athletic coach supervised the playground. I decided to go out for the basketball team, and I went all out. The coach gave me a place on the squad as a substitute. I was so thrilled that none of my sisters could talk to me, and Mamma could hardly catch me to do the household chores to which I had been assigned. I literally spent all day at the playground.

Making the squad is one thing and getting into a game is another. We played teams from other playgrounds in the city and many of the games were tough. As a result, I sat on the bench. The coach, however, was a pretty human sort of fellow; and in one game, either because we were so far ahead that it didn't matter, or because we had been so badly beaten that there was no hope, I got my chance. I played in the last three minutes of the final quarter, and I think I made one basket. I was a player on the team! Best of all, our team won some sort of championship. The regular players received medals, but there were not enough to go around to all the subs. However, the coach saw that I got one—a gold medal he had won himself once, for broad jumping.

About this time I discovered that I was a natural swimmer; buoyancy was one of the compensations for my underdeveloped little legs. One of the things I enjoyed most was swimming at the YMCA. I wore a pair of boys' sneakers to and from the pool on my misshapen stumps and always picked a time when the pool was likely to be empty.

Carried along on this wave of enthusiasm for athletics, I found myself hanging around the gym and locker room that fall when I went on to Newtown High School. I always turned up at basketball practice. I liked the smell of leather, and soap and steam on healthy flesh, and the casual goodfellowship of ribald locker-room talk. Best of all, these boys accepted me.

I had become a good shot in basketball, but since my height was well under four feet I could hardly play in competition. However, I got a chance to coach a neighborhood team, and after we won a community championship it was an easy step to become manager of the high school basketball team.

There was a sense of insulation about "my team," as I thought of it. When I sat on the bench alongside the coach, clocking the game and keeping statistics, I felt safe. These big strong men were my friends. They protected me from the world.

In a way, the athletes even helped me to face the world, because it was through my association with them that I earned my first money.

One afternoon when I had walked up from the streetcar that brought me from school, Mamma met me at the front door, her eyes bright but somewhat puzzled.

"A man called you on the telephone," she said before I reached the steps. "He wants you to call him back. It's *The New York Times*. Has anything gone wrong at school?"

As mystified as Mamma, I called the number.

"This is Gebhart on the sports desk," a voice said. "You Viscardi?"

"Yes, sir."

"We need a man at your school to phone in the results of the basketball games. We'll pay you a line rate for what we use. Are you interested?"

Was I *interested?* This was something I had never dreamed of. I was to report our basketball games to the *Times,* and be *paid* for it—

"Mamma, I've got a job."

She bent down and kissed me.

So that is how, ironically enough, I got my first job as a "leg man." Every night after the game I phoned in the score, the lineup, the fouls, and then next morning I hurried down to the newsstand to see my "story" in print. I don't remember what the remuneration was, but money could not have paid me as well as the satisfaction of doing something useful.

Through participation in athletics, I found another way to supplement the family income. It was refereeing basketball games—three dollars a game in the church leagues, and twelve dollars for semi-"pro" games. It kept me busy, but, as it later developed, was the beginning of a strain that proved to be almost more than my inadequate stumps could take.

The world of the high school was always a strange one. It was jammed beyond capacity and ran on four shifts. New roads and houses were being built as swarms of families moved into Queens. Raymond, the boy next door, gave up the struggle completely. Coping with the crowded streetcars and the forbidding stairways was too much for him. He dropped out of school.

"It is too bad," Mamma kept saying. "A boy like that will need all the education he can get."

Except for my charmed circle of athletes, I knew few students. Once in a while I would go to the candy store across the street from school where they gathered for Cokes and whatever items of food that were not tabooed by the coach. The girls gathered there too; they were girls in name only— I doubt if a wiser group of young ladies was ever collected in one place. They were *officially* taboo for the athletes, at least during season, and were certainly taboo for me because I was not interested in girls. And they obviously were getting along all right without me. I left them to the athletes and took my *Times* sports page and coffee to a quiet corner, where I read in the most blasé manner I could affect.

Our team won the New York City championship the year I was a senior. This made it possible for me to receive a major letter from the school for "Excellence in Athletics," along with a gold basketball medal. Another thrill came with my election to Arista, a high-school honor society, because of my grades. Somewhere along the way I won an annual extemporaneous speaking contest—the subject I drew was, of all things, "My Brother's Keeper."

Although my circle of friends was small, it was natural that because of my short stature I should become well known. As a result I was made an officer of the student government association, but the political plum I really craved was the presidency of the senior class.

Lacking the political know-how, or perhaps the desire, to acquaint my classmates with my interest in this office, I went to the class election meeting without having arranged for anyone to nominate me. I guess I expected the job to fall in my lap.

Well, it didn't.

Someone nominated a boy whose chief claim to distinction was that his father owned a lot of real estate and bank stock. The group was lethargic. Nobody else got up to make a nomination. Why doesn't somebody nominate me? I thought. I concentrated hard on it, but no one did. Then I heard the chairman say ". . . if there are no further nominations—"

This is terrible, I thought. Why doesn't somebody nominate *somebody*?

". . . do I hear a motion that the nominations be closed?"

I was on my feet, leaning out into the aisle so that I could be seen. "Mr. Chairman, I'd like to nominate Billy Jackson."

If I could not have the job myself, Bill was the man I wanted to see elected. He was an excellent student, popular, and a decent guy. I made an impassioned speech, defining those qualities in oratorical terms, and sat down.

The day was saved. The opponent from the right side of the tracks went down to defeat on the first ballot, and my man won—by an overwhelming majority, which surprised both him and me. His victory was so unprecedented that I was called down by two reactionary faculty members and a New York tabloid headlined the story. You see, Bill Jackson was a Negro.

He was a good class president and he won a scholarship to Harvard the following year. . . .

One bright October day my last year in high school, Papa and I went out on the train to visit Gouldie, who was by this time living on the Island in a house that reminded me, in its daintiness and the fragility of its decoration, of Gouldie herself.

She kissed me on the cheek. "You're very grown up—now I hope I'm not embarrassing you."

After inquiring about Mamma and the girls, she poured tea for us and served brownies she had baked herself.

"You still have the china dog, I see."

This started Gouldie and myself on a long chain of memories of the hospital. While we talked, Papa entered the conversation now and then to mention an important stock he was supposedly investing in or to allude in a casual way to a prominent business executive. Gouldie was attentive to Papa's pronouncements, and acted as though she accepted him for the man of the world he wanted so much to be. He had a wonderful time that day.

"I remember the teapot, but where did that silver loving cup come from?" I asked Gouldie.

She laughed lightly. "Cardy, I'm surprised. Don't you *know?* That's the loving cup the children at the hospital gave me on my tenth anniversary. Some of your pennies went into it. It's my dearest possession."

When we left, promising to come back soon, I wondered how Gouldie had managed to stay the same through all the years.

It was an illusion though: Gouldie was not the same. A few months later we received a letter from her attorneys, advising us that she had died, suddenly but quietly, and that she had left me a small bequest in cash and the "silver loving cup presented to her by the patients of the Children's Ward of the Hospital for Deformities and Joint Diseases."

It does not seem possible that you could miss someone

whom you saw so rarely. But Gouldie had been more a part of my life than I realized. There was nothing I could do to dispel the feeling of emptiness. There was not even a person I could write to—to offer my condolences.

Paradoxically, though, Gouldie's legacy brought a glimmer of hope. For a long time I had been wanting to go to college. It was as much a desire to get away from home as to gain further education—not that I didn't love my family, but I was restless to get on, to prove myself if I could. I did not mention this at home; college was expensive and I should be helping to support the family. Terry had left high school to work as a beautician in Papa's shop, but the three other girls were still in school.

One night around Christmas time, I sat at the dining-room table after supper looking over some college catalogues I had borrowed from a friend. I would graduate in February. Maybe I could work until fall. With the money from Gouldie's bequest, and maybe a job to pay for my board and room I might— Oh, what's the use? I thought. I can't afford it. And then, college would mean a whole new world, new people to meet . . . The giants of my childhood were back.

I felt a hand on my shoulder and looked up.

"You want to go to college," Mamma said. "You should go."

I shook my head. "It would cost too much."

"You go," Mamma said. "We'll manage somehow."

I put my arm around her waist and gave her a big hug. "Why, Mamma," I said shakily, "you're crying."

4

The Cloister

Outside the high fence that surrounded the university were the rush of traffic and the life of a great city, the competitions and disappointments of day-to-day existence.

Inside was a world of philosophy and religion, of men who had devoted their lives to teaching and prayer, and young men united in a fellowship of learning. The competitions were games and intellectual controversies. It was a dream world, but it was very real to me.

Fordham University. All new. All exciting. All to be explored.

It was hard to realize that I was actually here, still staring up at the Gothic towers, the tall elms, or venturing down the terraced slopes into the rock gardens; meeting the quiet Jesuits as they walked purposefully through the campus, their belted cassocks swaying stiffly; or glimpsing them from the distance as they strolled on their shady porch reading their breviaries.

The business course with shorthand, which I had taken after graduation from high school, had made it possible for me to get a job in the treasurer's office. I was working in the freshman dining hall too, as a sort of busboy. And I had started lining up basketball games to referee later on.

Fordham had seemed a logical choice. It was close enough to cut travel expense to a minimum—one nickel on the Lexington Avenue Subway, with changes of trains at Grand Central and uptown. The battered trunk which Mamma had miraculously produced from some unknown family storage place, and the old oak rocker she had insisted on my having, would come by express.

I had told Mamma the rocking chair was not necessary—I was sure the rooms were furnished. But when she said, "I'm sorry—I thought it would be a touch of home," I laughed and said, "O.K., Mom, thanks a lot."

One of the requirements for entrance into Fordham was a physical examination, so during the summer I had gone back to Dr. Yanover. He had moved to a suite of offices in a professional building in Jackson Heights and now had a nurse. Although I had not seen him for some time, his firm handclasp and friendly greeting reassured me.

"Going to college, eh?" he said. He removed a stethoscope from the pocket of his well-cut sports jacket. "Let's see what shape you're in."

He gave me a complete checkup, and spent considerable time examining my stumps and asking questions. Though his waiting room was crowded with patients, he seemed in no hurry to have me leave. "Come back into the office when you're dressed. I'd like to have a talk with you."

As I knotted my tie I had a strange feeling. Suppose that Dr. Yanover had discovered something wrong with my legs? They had been swollen many times, particularly after the strenuous activity of refereeing a game; and they had given me a good bit of pain during the spring, so much so at times that I had had to bind them with elastic bandages. But then, there had always been pain. Doc had seemed as cheerful as ever, but I had an idea he was a pretty good actor. Suppose something would stop me from going to college? I wouldn't have it. I tightened the laces on my clumsy boots and went into his office.

Dr. Yanover sat at his desk tapping his pipe on a large ash tray. He grinned. "You've stayed away a long time, Hank."

I nodded. Why didn't he come out and say it?

"I have news for you."

"Yes—?" My voice sounded hoarse.

"You are in very good physical shape for a guy of nineteen. I can't find a thing wrong with you, organically."

I dared to breathe. "That's good news, Doc."

"Except . . . you've been running those legs of yours pretty hard, haven't you?"

I agreed.

"Treat them with a little respect. You're going to need them for a while."

Then we had a sort of man-to-man talk—about lots of things, and he asked about Mamma and the family. When I got up to leave, Dr. Yanover said, "You're taller, Hank."

"Not much." I tried not to sound bitter.

"That measuring stick in the examining room says so." He paused. "How would you like to be as tall as everyone else?"

I laughed. "You're just like Mamma, Doc. She took some flowers to church a couple of weeks ago on St. Anthony's feast day. She says he's going to see that I have real legs some day. It's a perpetual novena she's been making since I was born."

"Maybe she's right." Doc gave me a quick grin that was a mental pat on the back. "Promise to keep in touch with me while you're at school—and tell Mamma to keep the pressure on St. Anthony." . . .

I shifted the pile of catalogues and registration forms to my left hand and opened one of the double doors of Collins Hall. The Freshman Meeting had already started. "All right, fellows," a self-assured young man on the platform was saying, "take off your jackets and turn them wrong-side out." There was a shuffling of feet and a banging of books as the hall full of entering students got up to comply.

I slipped into the last row, which was empty, set down my stack of things, and took off my coat, carefully turning the lining out.

"Remember now, you're to wear 'em this way all day. Any frosh caught disobeying rules—well, all I can say is we have a very competent committee here." The speaker nodded to the row of huskies lined up beside him. Each one carried a wooden paddle a yard long and an inch thick. Gee, I thought, those guys can't be sophomores. They must have hired them from a strong men's act at Loew's.

"You—down there," the chairman pointed to a frosh in the third row, "what are you laughing at? Get up."

"I wasn't laughing." The boy sounded defiant, although he was a stringy-looking kid, and poorly insulated for paddling.

"Come on up here—you, too."

This started a free-for-all, except that only the whacks from the paddles of the committee were free. The freshmen who resisted got it twice as hard. Everybody in the place got it eventually.

That is, practically everybody. They didn't paddle me.

When I was leaving with the others, the chairman passed me. His smile was friendly. "I hope you enjoyed it."

Suddenly I remembered a scared little kid hobbling into a schoolyard on 101st Street the first day of the term. The rules had changed.

I looked at the clock in the corridor. Eleven thirty. I was due in the dining hall.

The aging charm of Fordham extended inside the college buildings, particularly the chapel with its numerous altars, saints' windows, and shrines where votive lights flickered; and the administration building where the corridors were lined, almost frame to frame, with mellowed oil portraits of past Jesuit faculty members. However, at the doors of the students' rooms, charm withdrew and only age entered. I was assigned to one of these cell-like setups with cot beds, pancake mattresses, and jail-gray blankets; and the inadequate chests and battered desk that seemed to be standard equipment in college dorms. It was on the third floor of Dealy Hall, which housed all freshmen, along with the dining halls, billiard room, mailboxes, and some classrooms.

My roommate was a tawny giant named Stanley Maximowicz, from Buffalo. He was a scholarship man who had played brilliant football in high school and was a sure thing from the day they persuaded him to come to Fordham. The Fordham squad at that time, like the "Irish of Notre Dame," was distinguished by such names as Bomwitsky, Grabowsky, etc. Stan and I established a cordial relationship from the start, based mostly on a disinterested tolerance for each other's activities.

My schedule of jobs and classes—I had decided to major in sciences so would have many hours of lab—kept me out of the room practically all day, when presumably Stan was either at scrimmage or enjoying the room's solitude flexing his biceps and sleeping. For his social activities made heavy inroads into the hours set aside by the university for the latter purpose. Early in the year he established a wide circle of young women friends in Mount Vernon and other easily accessible communities, where he was in the habit of visiting after the "lights out" hour.

On week nights we were required to be in our rooms at seven thirty to begin the study period. At ten we assembled in the main corridor on our floor for prayers led by the Jesuit prefect in charge. After ten thirty the "Jebby" (as he was referred to in Fordham slang) checked the rooms to be sure everyone was in bed.

One night, immediately after prayers, Maximowicz, in accordance with his usual custom, put a dummy made of pillows and football jerseys into his bed, dressed in his "dating" clothes, complete in every detail except for his shoes, which he carried in one hand, and tiptoed out after checking to see that the coast was clear. I threw open the window in a hopeless effort to rid the room of the heady smell of the cologne Maximowicz affected, switched off the light, and climbed up into bed.

But sleep did not come immediately. In about three minutes there was a rattling of the doorknob, a massive figure galloped across the room, and Stan hissed, "Close the door— close the door!"

I slid off my cot, worked my way over to the door, and leaned. Somebody was pushing from the other side. I could hear Stan cursing as he tore at his bed. I held the door as long as I could. Then it flew open with me behind it. The light clicked on and the prefect called from the doorway, "Mr. Maximowicz, you look very peculiar indeed."

Stan was sitting up in bed trying to pull the covers around him. He was completely dressed, even to topcoat and derby.

The Jebby then pulled back the door and turned to me, frozen in my niche. "Mr. Viscardi, is that where you sleep?" But the corner of his mouth was twitching.

One of my pleasantest memories of Fordham is associated with the assemblies in the courtyard during the month of May, which is dedicated to the Blessed Lady. Every day just before lunch the entire student body gathered for a few minutes around the statue of the Blessed Virgin, where a vigil light burned, to hear a student deliver a short sermon. Then we sang the *Regina Coeli Laetare*. On the days when I had to be in the dining hall I could hear the mellow voices swelling in chorus through the open windows:

> "*Regina coeli laetare,*
> *Al-le-luia! Al-le-luia!*
> *Regina coeli laetare,*
> *Al-le-luia, Al-le-luia!*
> *Qui aquem . . .*"

It was warm and wonderful, and for the first time in my life I felt a thrilling awe and reverence in my religion.

The privilege of visiting the chapel often was one that I really appreciated. We had lived so far from the parish church in Elmhurst that I had become a rather infrequent participant. At Fordham one could hear Masses being celebrated at any time in the morning, as the Jebbies fulfilled their daily obligations; or one could pause for a few minutes of quiet during a busy afternoon.

At Mass a Jesuit lay brother or a student often served for the priest, but sometimes there was no one to assist. One morning the thought occurred to me that perhaps I could do this. How could you manage up there, I kidded myself, tottering around with the missal? But the idea stayed.

That noon, just after I had put the bread plates on a table and was turning up the water glasses, the brother who had charge of the dining halls and chapel came in. I went over and spoke to him.

"Brother Quinn, I've been wondering if you could use any help in serving Mass. If so, I'd like to try."

"Why, of course, young man. Meet me in the sacristy this afternoon."

My new duties meant that I had to get up every day shortly after five to serve my first Mass at a quarter to six. I loved crossing the quiet campus on early spring mornings, through the courtyard where the small vigil light burned and the statue of the Blessed Virgin was tinted a pale rose. Then to the chapel, where the blue and gold stained-glass windows which faced the east gradually lighted up, as I said my prayers at the kneeling bench in the sacristy.

At first I wore the lace surplice over my suit coat. It hung to my waist. Soon, however, Brother Quinn found a black cassock which fitted me perfectly through the shoulders. "You may keep this," he said. "Perhaps someone could shorten it."

"I know just the person."

Mamma was thrilled when I wrote to her, and the cassock came back almost by return mail, neatly shortened and hemmed. With my own cassock and the soft, pure-feeling surplice over it, I was the proudest student in Fordham. How wonderful it would be if I could enter the priesthood!

My first Mass was served for Father Fay, a rather austere young priest who always thanked me politely at the end, but never engaged me in conversation. Quite often I served a second Mass too. Generally, I helped at one of the six side altars, which had only one step, but once when the brother who served was absent I filled in for him at the higher center altar, where there were more steps. Father Azmuth, the massive and rather terrifying biology teacher, was the celebrant. In his vestments he seemed to tower a good seven feet. The center altar was the only one with electric chimes. These seemed a more majestic supplement to Father Azmuth's rumbling voice than the Mass bell, so at the first opportunity I sounded them. The reprimand was quick and unmistakable: "Do *not* ring those chimes!"

We finished with the tinkling Mass bell. It was comforting to realize that the church was dark and empty as the student Mass would not take place until later.

The Mass book was unusually heavy that day as I hoisted it up and down the steps and did all the extra walking required by the large altar. This rather hazardous experience was good preparation, though, for a time many years later. During World War II, I was called upon to help a wounded Catholic chaplain learn to use an artificial limb in walking and performing the duties of his office.

At the beginning of the second year Stan moved in with another football player down the hall and I was to have a new roommate, Bill Nash. So I was quite surprised when I went up to my room before dinner on registration day to see a strange boy sitting on a trunk in the middle of the floor, as matter-of-factly as though he were waiting in Grand Central Station for a train to Pelham. He was long and lean and his checked suit was of an expensive material.

"Hello. What are you doing here?" I said.

"Just resting, old chap. I understand I'm to live here."

"That's strange. I had been assigned someone else."

"Quite all right, old boy. Mind if I stay for the time being?" He extracted a cigarette from a flat package and carefully inserted it in a long holder.

"No, I guess not. Except I hate to tell you to unpack your things until you know definitely. You're new, aren't you?"

"Yes. John Orindoff. From London, Ontario. '*Payter*' liked the sound of this place."

John stayed; Nash had been assigned to another place at the last minute.

We roomed together all through college. Considering the

difference in our backgrounds, it was odd that we became such good friends. Between us we worked out a fairly effective schedule. The first of the month when Pater's generous check came, John and I went on a spending spree—movies in town, food—then the rest of the month we lived off my earnings. So we were either wealthy or broke together.

If it had not been for John I would never have tackled the problem of the biology smock. Though he was majoring in chemistry, we both took biology from Father Azmuth during our sophomore year.

In addition to his commanding stature, which was so apparent when he celebrated Mass at the center altar, Father Azmuth possessed a big belly and a black beard and a small bald spot on top of his head. With a Prussian disdain for the common things of life, he confined his conversation with students to few words. The most frequent personal remark Father Azmuth directed to one of his young men—this was usually addressed to those slouching, sleeping, or chewing gum during lectures—was "A-a-*out!* Leave this classroom!"

Lab periods furnished a pleasant break in the class routine. We were required to wear tan smocks which we had to purchase in the campus bookstore.

"And vear them Monday. Not Vensday—Monday," Father Azmuth warned as we filed out of class. John and I got our smocks and took them up to our room. Though mine was the smallest size in stock and I thought my shoulders were going to bust it out, it was still about a yard too long.

"Gee, I can never get this smock to Mamma and back before Monday," I said.

"Don't worry, old boy. We can fix it." John went to the top drawer and took out a spool of heavy black thread and a big needle. I did not realize at first that what John meant was that I would fix the smock under his direction. This was accomplished by spreading it out on my bed and folding it under. Then, when John had succeeded in threading the needle, I went to work. A couple of hours later the final stitch was taken and I looked at my achievement with pride.

"Try it on, Hank," he suggested.

I picked up the smock—but the spread came with it. I had sewed it right to the bed.

John frowned for a minute, went out the door, and came back with a pair of shears. Neatly he clipped off the threads. But it was obvious the hem would not stay in, so finally we cut it off all the way around. In trying to even it up, John made one side a little too short, and the result was an interesting uneven hemline. The black threads and part of the smock stayed in my bedspread all semester.

When we went to lab on Monday, John managed to keep between me and Father Azmuth. We had succeeded very well until about five minutes before the end of the period, when Father Azmuth came by my lab bench to have a look at his cage of white mice. He stopped suddenly and stared down at me. His face reddened. It went almost purple. From the corner of my eye I saw John stop halfway across the room with a scalpel upraised in his hand. I sent him a telepathic message which was not exactly a love note.

"Vot hass happened with your smock? Ho-ho-ho!" Father Azmuth's bass laugh rolled out and made the test tubes rattle all over the lab. "Dot's good. Very good."

John and I had a good neighbor in the person of "Dutch" Folser, who lived across the hall. This athletic young man was properly referred to as Mr. John Folser, S.J. He was a scholastic, who was going through his required period of teaching and study before he was ordained as a priest. Like most of the other Jebbies, Mr. Folser was a nice guy. He didn't mind your calling him "Dutch" as long as you didn't do it to his face. On Saturday nights when most of the boys had gone out on dates, or on Sunday afternoons when they walked with their girls along the avenue of elm trees at the end of the campus, I used to sit and talk to Dutch about history and religion and philosophy.

One time I confided my interest in the priesthood to him.

"A worthy desire," he said. "Are you sure that's what you really want to do?"

"Of course, but . . ." In Dutch's cheerful face, which had suddenly become serious, I saw the answer to my question. "They wouldn't take me, would they?"

"Some of the regulations of the Church may seem harsh, Hank. But there's always a reason. A priest's duties may take him anywhere. So he has to pass a rigid physical examination. Even a man with heart trouble would have a hard time getting into most of the orders."

"Perhaps I'll be a teacher," I went on quickly. But there was no real ring to the words. I knew only that I wanted to stay here in this quiet place and study and meditate.

Even if I had the inclination to venture outside the university grounds, my busy schedule would have given me little opportunity. Summers I stayed at Fordham and worked full time in the offices in an effort to keep pace with the bills that kept piling up. It seemed I always owed the university money —for last term's room, next term's tuition, a long overdue lab fee—always something. Winters I went to school. Here and there I found ways to earn an extra five dollars or so to help meet expenses. I worked in the library part time. I learned to operate the college switchboard. I became acquainted with a student who had been trained as a barber and traded themes for haircuts. One term I paid my tuition by transcribing my shorthand lecture notes in Qualitative Analysis and having them printed to sell to new students. This transaction had the blessing of the professor since there was no textbook for the course.

In addition to my refereeing of basketball games, I made one or two other attempts at athletic jobs. These were not entirely successful, particularly the first one. Word spread across the campus one day that at noon they would sign up men over at our athletic field to work at the Polo Grounds. We would have to sell programs, act as ushers, etc. I went over when I had finished work in the dining hall. The line in front of the ticket booth was quite long. I got on the end, and no one came after me. They seemed to be signing up everybody, but when I reached the booth, the man inside stared down at me. "Sorry, bud, the jobs are all taken." He closed the window.

I picked up a stone and hurled it hard across the field. Then I pounded through the campus to the dorm. I had to stop on the second floor and rest; my legs were throbbing with pain. I had to admit, too, that maybe the man was right. What about the cash customers at the ball park—would they want such an usher?

One spring Father Fitzpatrick, the Jebby in charge of the athletic field, gave me the job of running the new baseball scoreboard, at five dollars per game. It was attached to a wall of the gym over in deep left field, and was similar in design to the one used at the Polo Grounds. A huge metal affair, it was operated from within by an intricate system of sash-weighted cords on pulleys, which hauled numerals on its face up and down to indicate balls, strikes, runs, and the other statistics of the game.

The first three games went fine. From my peephole inside the scoreboard I was able to hoist the various numerals into position without too many errors. The fourth game, with Columbia, our big rival, was preceded by two days of heavy rain. When I got to my perch just before game time I dis- covered that the ropes had become so shrunk I couldn't work them at all. Dame Fortune smiled that day, but not on me. She gave the Columbia team a revolutionary lucky streak in the first inning and they chalked up three home runs—one with the bases loaded. I was still trying to untangle the mess of ropes. As a further complication, one of the runs was dis- puted, so at the end of the inning all eyes turned to the score- board, including Father Fitzpatrick's. Instead of the score, he and the anxious fans saw my head protruding from the square slot.

"What's the score, anyhow?" I shouted.

"You're fired!" Father Fitz answered. But he relented later.

When I think of the years at Fordham, I remember best the bull sessions with Dutch Folser. These often included John, who found social life less attractive than the idea of getting good grades. Sometimes Dutch would stick his head in our room between periods of correcting freshman themes and reading his office. He always carefully averted his face when John's illegal hot plate was plugged in.

"Someone must be making coffee down in the cafeteria," he would say, sniffing elaborately. And if we had our Satur- day night snack before twelve o'clock when his fast started, Dutch would munch delightedly on one of the foot-square sandwiches we concocted from pumpernickel bread and other tidbits from the kosher delicatessen outside the grounds on Fordham Road.

The night Prohibition was repealed occurred in my junior year. John and I got half a dozen bottles of watery beer, and iced them in Dutch's bathtub. They were opened and passed around before the beer was really cold.

"Here's to your health, gentlemen," Dutch said.

I looked at Dutch and I looked at John, and I was very

grown up as I drank my beer. For a moment I forgot that there was another life waiting outside—a life to which I eventually must return.

How soon I would return to the other life I did not realize. At the end of that year I worked at Fordham through the summer as usual. Having a few free days in September before the fall term started, I went home to visit Mamma and the girls.

Then the letter came. I read it three times before the full meaning impressed itself upon me. It was from the treasurer's office. They regretted to inform me that unless I paid up all outstanding bills immediately I could not enroll in the fall term. I couldn't go back to school. There was no question of my paying. I did not have the money. By the middle of the year I might, but at the time, no.

Carefully I folded the letter and creased it, then folded it again, and again. When it was a small packet I slipped it down into my inside pocket. But I couldn't forget that it was there. And I knew that I couldn't put off telling Mamma.

A memory of Stan Maximówicz dressed in his dating clothes galloped through my mind.

Too bad, I thought, that I wasn't born an athlete like Stan. Then I could get through college on a scholarship.

5

Attorneys and Counselors

It was the black pit of the subway with its sour smell—a subway peopled with pushing, shoving giants. They were not the terrifying giants of my childhood but they were still distasteful to me.

There were the thick-skinned ones, who stared like hill people come down to see a traveling show. There were the paper-peekers, the furtive kind who would withdraw blushing if you caught them at it. There were the pitying ones, whose tongue clickings could almost be heard after they had passed you. But even worse, there were the chatterers, whose every remark might as well have been "How do you do, poor boy?" They said it with their eyes and their manners and their tone of voice.

I had a standard defense—a cold stare. Thus anesthetized against my fellow man, I could contend with the basic problem—getting in and out of the subway alive. Catastrophe hid in daylight on slippery stairs. Suffocation was not far off in the crowded passages for a man not four feet tall, and death lurked at every trackside waiting for a careless step.

Once on the train, the sudden swoosh of the wheezy door

was a signal of new perils to come. I clutched whatever was at hand—one of the bars at the center of the car or, failing that, the corner of a seat. The "straps," whose porcelain finish was redolent of a city hospital or a public washroom, were well beyond my reach. I fought to stay near the door, for once in the center of the car, I was in physical and mental peril from the unseeing horde of people so tall they rarely noticed me. There was absolutely nothing to hang on to, and I had no knees to flex against the shipboard sort of swaying of the noisy rushing train.

But there is something essentially challenging in the fight for physical safety, even though it be waged in such sordid surroundings. With the proper philosophy you can make it into an absorbing game. The enemy was visible, I knew what my resources were, and my chances of survival.

The game ends, though, when you find yourself lacking the weapons with which to fight. For I was engaged in a more serious battle—for self-sufficiency, human dignity, the restoration of my sense-of-self, call it what you will—I was looking for a job. And these were depression years. I had no weapons.

The train disgorged a mass of us at a midtown station, and I glanced again at the address of the employment agency I would "visit" today, trying to memorize the address: it was on Forty-third Street between Fifth and Sixth avenues. A dried-up-looking man came by and took my arm. Despite my unresponsiveness, he drew me up a flight of stairs and all the way out of the station where he deposited me with a sanctimonious smile on the wrong side of the street.

Mother of God, I thought, I bet he's the kind who goes to church and prays for those poor helpless cripples.

The agency looked like most of them except that it was more crowded. Lines of people were spread all over a large room—crossing, recrossing, and intermingling. Department-store boys wearing carefully polished shoes, fashionable ties, and home-pressed trousers of good cut, rubbed shoulders with stringy women stenographers; and young college graduates of my age filled out white cards at counters shared by middle-aged business men in seedy-looking suits.

Along the walls were posted signs: MALE, FEMALE, $10, $15, $25. Quickly finding my level, I got into the line under MALE—$10. The oppressive atmosphere of the room gave me a headache, and the medley of noise was so thick that only an occasional phrase bobbed to the surface of the alphabet soup. You heard such bits as "They say the government is hiring again. . . . No, not NRA, a new agency," or "Gert got a job at United." "How nauseous—me, I'd rather starve."

Fordham seemed very far behind me, much further than a month.

By noon I had gotten almost to the desk. My line was moving slowly, and the clerk was bobbing, interviewing, telephoning, repeating questions and gestures like a mechanical doll with frizzy hair and chipped nail polish. Some applicants got white cards to fill out over at one of the long counters. Some got a shrug of the shoulders or a dry retort.

My interview did not take long. "I have a university ed—" My chin seemed scarcely six inches above the desk top.

"Sorry, we have nothing for you."

Anyway I would not have to worry about reaching up to the counter to fill out my card.

Then, through some gust of fate, or maybe a pitchman's whim, the Wheel of Fortune clicked along a couple of more notches and came to a stop at my number. The prize I drew was The Law. I had heard about the job through a friend, and I started working toward the end of 1934 as a clerk in the law firm of Gellman and Gellman, which was located in Corona, right near home.

Sam and Joe Gellman, the partners, had private offices,

and Pop Gellman, who was in the real estate business, made room for me alongside his desk out in the reception room. The corner which Pop referred to as our "office" was busy with clients coming and going; with wrongs to be righted, deeds to be examined, wills to be drawn, and the clerical and research jobs either jovial Sam or his quieter younger brother Joe passed on to me. The ten-dollar weekly salary which I received would certainly help out at home.

Mamma was alone now, with us children: Papa was dead. Terry continued her work as a beautician. Lil had graduated and married her high school sweetheart. Vicky and Rose were still in school and I wanted them to finish.

I was being paid for one of my favorite pastimes, reading. And what reading! I sampled everything from British Common Law to Corpus Juris. At the end of the first week, Pop said, "Do you like the law, boy?"

"I think I'm going to like it a lot. It's all so new of course —Joe promised to take me to court next week."

"Good, good," Pop said.

It was a busy life. In addition to their active criminal practice the Gellmans handled a considerable amount of property litigation. Many of the new homes that had been built a few years earlier were now changing hands via foreclosures or sales, as their original owners found they could no longer make the payments.

As time passed I learned to examine titles and abstracts, in addition to looking up law and helping to prepare briefs. In this new world, I worked and I learned.

And I became acquainted with an eminent member of the legal profession—Mr. Ephraim Tutt, Arthur Train's character in the *Saturday Evening Post* stories. Here was the personification of the highest legal standards, tempered by humor and horse sense. I tried the part and it fitted. In the intermingling of my ideals with those of my hero, I absorbed

many of the Tutt mannerisms, probably the most outstanding of which was his preference for Marsh Wheeling stogies.
I took to keeping them in my desk drawer and lighting one
of the long black things when I sat down to read the law.

My interest in this field was rapidly assuming much more
than casual proportions. Why not go to school and study law?
Maybe I could find a way to earn some extra money to pay
my tuition.

The chief disadvantage of my new routine was that I had
to commute every night on the subway to St. John's University in Brooklyn, where I took law classes from seven to nine.
Although I made an effort to ride on the same car every
evening, so that at least some of the passengers would become
accustomed to me, it helped little. There were still rude
stares and clumsy efforts at assistance. Since it was usually
possible to get a seat at this hour, I did manage to read law
on the train. With my evening classes on top of my daytime
job, my schedule was a heavy one—I often fell asleep in class.

Through the registration office at the university, I got a
chance to earn the extra money I needed. An orthodox Jewish student who attended the graduate school had a Saturday
lecture in Bankruptcy Law. Due to his strict adherence to his
religion, he was not permitted to write on the Sabbath. So it
was arranged that I should attend lectures with him and take
his notes.

During these dog-eat-dog days of subway riding I had
adopted an attitude of hostility toward all strangers, and
Myron Kantor was no exception. I insisted on being paid my
weekly compensation at the close of each lecture. He was
equally insistent that I not be paid at that time—he could
not handle money on the Sabbath either. We carried our
problem, with violent gestures and heated declamations, to
the bursar's office.

"What's all the fuss about?" The speaker was a petite blonde with an Irish twinkle. I blushed, and suddenly felt foolish.

"Why don't you arrange it this way? You"—she gestured toward me—"call here every Saturday after class and I'll pay you. Then Mr. Kantor can stop in on Monday and reimburse *me*."

"You mean out of your own pocket?" I said.

She shrugged her small shoulders and smiled. "I've financed lots of deals. You get used to handling money in this place."

As the course progressed, another problem came up. It was apparent that since Kantor could not take lecture notes he would not be able to write exams either. The professor called us in to discuss it. "This is highly irregular," he said. "There would be nothing to prevent Mr. Viscardi from helping you, Mr. Kantor, to answer a question that seemed to be difficult." Nothing, I thought, except my lack of love for my employer.

"We are not friends, it is just a business arrangement," I assured the professor afterward.

"Try it on Saturday and see how it works."

The fact was that Kantor had taken a similar dislike to me. That made it even funnier for the two of us to be sitting conspiratorially off in a corner during exams while he whispered to me what to write on his paper and then watched closely to see that I did it.

In spite of this mutual unlove, our arrangement lasted throughout the year. Kantor would have had trouble finding another law student who could take complete lecture notes, as I could, in shorthand if necessary. On my part, I needed the money. Besides, I was getting a chance at strictly graduate courses to which I would never have had access otherwise.

To fill out the week, I studied on Sunday with two other students in a law office in downtown Manhattan where one of them worked. Sitting in the snug library at the big table with my friends beside me, the pungent leather-bound law books surrounding us, and two or three of Eph Tutt's stogies in my pocket, I felt safe and certain again. This study of law was fascinating and important.

As I progressed through the three-year course at St. John's, though, I sometimes wondered whether I was really interested in practicing law—in perhaps sometime having to defend a gangster—or whether I merely wanted to lose myself in the theory and philosophy of law.

When the federal government started the Home Owners' Loan Corporation, Gellman and Gellman were given a good share of local business to handle. Joe had been turning a lot of this title work over to me. I found that my interest in research, in tracking down elusive bits of information, really blossomed in these pursuits.

One day Joe said, "How do you like this phase of the work, Hank?"

"Fine."

"We've been told," he confided, "that it will be necessary to open an office in the Empire State Building to handle our HOLC business. They want us nearer to the regional office. Shall we go over?"

"It sounds good, Joe."

"I think we can pay you a better salary, too."

That really sounded good. I was almost a lawyer. I was going to have an office with Joe in the Empire State Building. Mamma and the girls would be proud.

It was just a cubicle partitioned into two rooms, but to me it was a palace. I loved it there. Within a short time, Joe was letting me handle most of the work and he began spending longer periods out in Corona.

I was in a busy dream. Office, night school, study—and it was all worth while. I now spent hours in the subway, but bolstered by my new feeling of self-worth, I minded it less. My glassy stare-down for the other passengers was no longer defensive, but rather the conditioned reflex of a busy professional man who could not be bothered exchanging pleasantries with annoying persons.

As usual, however, there was a new problem.

I had learned how to get along with girls—I left them alone—but I had no defense against Miss Trimble. She was the motherly spinster the HOLC had assigned to our office as secretary, and she undertook me as her special assignment.

She brought me cookies. She knitted me ear muffs. And mittens to match. She fretted that I was taking too much work home. She prescribed remedies when I appeared to be coming down with a cold. In short, she scared me to death.

She did her hair in a cabbage knot and affected a corseted style that my sister Terry said must have belonged to about 1910—a column of tight-laced foundation with an emancipated bosom topside. Possessed of this remarkable physical appearance and brimming over with kindness, the woman had a terrifying habit of being ever-present in my office with a stenographic notebook in hand, and the eager question, "Is there anything I can *do* for you?"

I was completely tongue-tied when she was in the room. So I took to writing all my letters and legal papers out in longhand first on a big yellow tablet. Then, when she came in, I would lay my hand casually across the tablet and take sidelong looks at it while I pretended to be dictating.

But I never did solve the problem of Miss Trimble herself. And I lived in dread of the day when she would enfold me in her arms and call me her little boy.

Jessie Barnes, on the other hand, was quite different. She was a government investigator with dyed red hair who had an office down the hall. She did a man's work and talked like a man, but she was all woman and didn't care who knew it.

I liked Jessie because you never had to worry about what you said to her, and because she was a friendly human being. She would lean on my desk and say, "How are you, kid?" and I would not have been surprised to see her light up one of my Marsh Wheeling stogies any day.

One afternoon when she had banged into my place for an exchange of social repartee, she was more effusive than usual.

"You're a smart boy," she said. "How would you like a new job?"

"What's your proposition, Jessie?"

Then she told me the HOLC was going to hire a bunch of tax clerks. She'd had a tip. And the jobs paid $1,500 a year. I was a natural for it, she said, with my experience, and "you know the Gellmans. They'd be glad to see you get ahead."

"There's a hooker to it of course," she went on. "You'll have to get an endorsement—you a democrat?"

I told her that I wasn't anything.

"Ump-unh—the man to see is Jerry Casey. I'll help you get your application through the office. I've got a friend in the personnel department." This was no lie. Jessie had a friend in every department.

Joe advised me to apply for the job. "It won't hurt, Hank, and you might get it. Run out and see Jerry Casey."

When I reached the Tammany clubhouse where Jerry Casey presided, I was ushered—by following a voice that called "Yeah?" from an unseen corner—into a cigar-butt-strewn cubbyhole in the back. A pair of large feet rested on the desk and greeted me, sole on, as I entered the presence of Mr. Casey himself.

The feet parted and I saw his distant flushed face. He removed a wet-looking cigar from his mouth.

"Who're you? Whatta ya want?"

It was hard to picture young party workers running errands on behalf of good government at the direction of the figure who was so completely relaxed in the swivel chair behind the desk.

I took a deep breath. "Mr. Casey, I'm an associate of Joe Gellman's. . . ." And I told him my story, finishing rather anxiously with "Would you give me your endorsement for the job? I'm sure I have good qualifications."

Mr. Casey looked at me over his feet. "That's nice, sonny. You a member of this club?"

The question was purely academic, but it was difficult to associate the man behind the desk with even the word.

"No."

"Whatja ever do for me?"

"Not a thing. How could I? I've never seen you before."

"Well, sonny, I'm gonna return the favor." He spat into an unseen cuspidor. "That's what I'm gonna do for *you*— nothing."

He closed his feet and the interview was at an end.

When I told Joe about it, he said, "I was afraid that would happen."

"But, Joe, why should a guy like Casey pass on my qualifications for a job? Doesn't my background mean anything?"

"It's politics, Hank. Now I'd suggest, if you're really interested, you start doing little party jobs in your district. Volunteer—telephone voters, distribute literature. Maybe in a couple of years you'll get an HOLC job—or another one."

"Are you kidding?" I said.

"No, I wish I were. Send your application in anyway," he said suddenly.

So I followed his advice.

I wanted the job, but my chances seemed so slim that it was quite a surprise one day several weeks later when the HOLC telephoned and asked me to come for an interview.

It turned out to be a series of interviews, at desks plotted

over the barnlike office of the HOLC that took up one floor
of the Empire State Building. The last interview occurred at
three A.M. with a tired administrator from Washington who
was in town for a conference.

Jessie phoned me a few days later. "You're in, kid. They'll
be calling you soon. Good luck. . . . Forget it, you can buy me
a drink sometime."

Joe would not let me turn in my key to the office. "You'll
always be part of the firm," he said. "If you ever want to
come back, remember there's a place for you."

Pop Gellman gave me a box of Marsh Wheeling stogies.

For a minute I did not want to leave.

Anyone who worked for one of the governmental alphabet
agencies that sprung up during the thirties will recall the
turmoil, the transitory offices, the confusion, the bookkeeping
snafus that resulted in long-overdue paychecks, the long waits
to go ahead with a new program; then the sudden pressure
once the appropriation for the new filing system or the five
hundred stenographers was voted through. The HOLC followed this general pattern, although I think it managed to
do a creditable job of helping individuals and stemming de-
flationary pressures during the years of its existence. While
I worked there, we occupied two locations besides the Empire State Building—one of these was on Park Avenue and
the other was in the McGraw-Hill Building, that square
tower of green metal and glass on West Forty-second Street.

I should have realized that my legs would suffer from the
strain I was putting them to. They were swelling quite often,
and the elastic bandages which had brought me some relief in
the Fordham days were only painful and binding now. Mornings I could hardly get my boots on. Sometimes it seemed as
though I would not get through my classes at night.

I needed something to help me get around—something like the coaster wagon in which I had taken Vicky to Dr. Yanover's office so long ago. How about a car?

The idea was absurd. The Viscardis were eating and my lavish (for those days) $1,500 salary helped Mamma get a washing machine and a few things for the house; but there was no provision for an automobile in our budget, and a person like myself would need a specially built car anyway.

I had about made up my mind to let this stogie dream blow away when one night at supper Mamma mentioned that her cousin Joe, who worked in a garage over in Manhattan, had telephoned that he had received a letter from an uncle in Italy who asked to be remembered to Mamma.

She was talking about Cousin Joe the *mechanic*. I remembered him.

"Where is his garage?" I asked.

"Let's see . . ." Mamma said. "I'm sorry, I don't know. But he *lives* uptown. I have the address."

The following Sunday I rode up to 167th Street and talked to Joe. He remembered me as a kid when we lived on 101st Street. Sure, he could get me a car. Not cheap though—"a hundred dollars maybe."

But could it be altered so that I could drive it?

"Don't worry. I'll fix it."

A week later he called me at work. "A nice car, Hank—I found it in Washington Heights. And a bargain. Only seventy-five dollars. . . . What kind is it? A very good car—Graham Paige, 1929 model."

"Isn't it worth more than that as an antique?" I said.

Joe laughed.

When he took me up to see the car, I bought it. With his peculiar mechanical genius he grafted long extensions on to clutch, brake, and accelerator, and added new pedals to these antennae. He also installed a pushbutton starter on the dash-board.

"You gotta fine car there, Hank. Motor runs good."

How "good" it would run would depend, I knew, on my mastery of it. Joe gave me three lessons the next week, and I decided to drive the buggy home.

"Without a license?" Joe said. "Hank, are you crazy?"

But I was not to be dissuaded. Taking my life in my hands —as well as my future as a licensed operator of motor vehicles in the state of New York—I started off. This was my first feeling of being normal. Behind the wheel I was the same as everyone else in the world—no different. It was great.

Two hours—and three near-collisions—later I drove up in front of the attached house in Elmhurst, and leaned on the horn. My repeated pressures brought out everyone in the block with much shouting and well-wishing, and finally Mamma, who rushed to the car.

There were shadows under her eyes and she looked frightened.

"Henry," she said, "what are you doing with a car?"

"It's mine, Mom. Cousin Joe got it for me."

"How can you drive it? Do you even have a license?"

Mamma's fears were allayed when I applied for a license and passed the tests, and she finally agreed to venture out in the ancient sedan for a demonstration. When I took her marketing on Saturday, she was won over.

"It is an old car, but it runs well," she said. Then she sighed.

I looked at Mamma closely. She was pale and there was a tenseness about her eyes and mouth. "Are you upset? Mamma, do you feel bad?"

She smiled quickly. "Why do you ask that, Henry? I am all right."

6

St. Anthony Keeps His Bargain

Pain will stay hidden but not for long. For a while you may deceive others, but you cannot conceal it from yourself. Pain can be staccato and dramatic, or dull and unbearable in its constant pursuit. And pain can be insidious as it pauses and brings an instant of relief while it prepares to attack anew in unsuspected dimensions.

Pain that one has lived with for a lifetime can suddenly turn from a tolerated companion to an open enemy. At first it may only anger its victim but ultimately it can defeat him.

Such was the battle being waged against me.

The legs had been driven too hard: it was pain to walk; it was almost impossible to lace the boots against the swelling. The elastic bandages brought another kind of pain—cruel and binding.

If I had not been so plagued with my own problems I might have been more concerned that Sunday in the late fall of 1936 when Mamma got up from the breakfast table to reach for something in the cupboard and suddenly sat down with a little sigh.

"Vicky," she said, "will you please get the sugar bowl?"

Looking up from the business section of the Sunday paper, I noticed deep shadows under her eyes. There were little drops of moisture on her taut upper lip.

"Mamma, I wish you'd take things easy on week ends when we're all home," Terry said from her cap of done-up curls.

I hitched myself back in my chair, trying to find a more comfortable position. "How about coming for a ride in the country in my chariot today?" I put in.

"Maybe," Mamma said. "We'll see."

But then it rained. Later in the day I heard Vicky ask Mamma, "Why don't you go to see the doctor?"

Another time, several weeks later, I arrived home ahead of the girls and found Mamma sitting alone in the front room.

Her face was pale and calm and she had not bothered to turn on the lights.

"Mamma—what on earth is the matter?"

Her eyes were like darker shadows in the twilight of the room as she turned toward me.

"The doctor—I saw him today. He says I should have an operation." Mamma spoke calmly, not fearfully but with something beyond fear that implied a quiet submission to whatever ordeal might be awaiting her.

Pain jagged through my left leg. "An operation? That doesn't need to be bad. Lots of people have surgery—why look how many operations I had." Somehow, my cheeriness fell flat.

"He says I should see another doctor—a surgeon."

"Well, Mamma, if that's the case I think we'd better look up Dr. Yanover."

Dr. Yanover was now married and had acquired a reputation as a fine young surgeon. I made an appointment for Mamma and a few days later drove her to the gray stone house in Jackson Heights where he shared offices with two or three other doctors. On the way she sat quietly beside me, but there was a tenseness about her features.

While I was waiting for Mamma, Dr. Yanover called me into his office.

He stood up and waved toward a chair with his pipe. He puffed at it quietly for a minute, then said, "Your mother needs surgery—right away."

A calm professional tone overlay his usual warmth. I was brought up short from my preoccupation with a sudden sickly feeling.

"Is it serious?"

"There would be no point in my lying to you, Hank. Her condition is serious. But fortunately there's something we can do about it. It's a fairly routine operation from our standpoint. We see many patients like your mother—women who have had a number of children and have put off surgery for years. She can't wait much longer. You'd better get her to the hospital in a day or two."

Some of the strain was gone from Mamma's face as we rode home.

She was operated on at Parsons Hospital, but her convalescence was interrupted by the need for a second operation a short while later, and she was slow in regaining her strength. In time, though, Dr. Yanover advised me that she was improving and could probably come home in about a week.

On the appointed day I called back. "How about it, Doc? Can I go to the hospital and bring Mom home?"

"Yes, your mother is ready to leave the hospital, but I want to have a talk with you."

"About Mom?"

"No, about yourself. Will you come in to see me in a few days."

"Sure, Doc."

Then I forgot about it—until one day the pain in my limbs was so severe I could not walk. So I went to see him.

Doc was pleasant, but less jovial than usual. "I have been thinking about you quite a bit lately."

"Yes?"

"Your stumps have been giving you a lot of pain, haven't they?"

It was a statement, not a question. I could not evade Doc's sharp eyes.

"I haven't looked you over for a very long time—"

"Not since I went away to school."

"Why don't you let me give you a complete checkup?"

I agreed without enthusiasm. What good would it do? We couldn't grow new legs.

After a very careful examination, and a complete set of X-rays, Dr. Yanover called me back to his office.

His face was serious as he lighted his pipe.

"What's the story?" I said.

"I'm going to be honest, Hank. It's not good."

His eyes were clear and he looked directly at me. I'll always remember the blue wool tie he was wearing that day.

"Your legs are burned out."

It should not have surprised me. The legs had been put to severe trials. They had run twice the course a pair of normal legs would be expected to cover in twenty-five years. There had been long days in the woods and fields. They had walked miles. They had carried greater weight than they should have through long hours on the basketball courts and years on the campus at Fordham. They had climbed subway stairs and had been brutally treated by falls in the jostling crowds. They had taken me back and forth to classes at St. John's and in and out of the HOLC offices. They had been driven by my unquenchable thirst for everything that was prized in life, for everything that others experienced.

A wave of warmth suffused me. "What do you mean by burned out?" I temporized.

Dr. Yanover raised his broad shoulders slightly and shook his head. "You can't go on as you have."

His words were an icy hand on my shoulder which I tried to shake off. "You mean I'll have to take things easy—"

"I wish I could tell you that."

The cold was inside of me now, a hard core. Even my legs in their taut elastic bandages felt cold.

It is difficult to say who has the greater ordeal, the person who must deliver the bad news or the recipient. It is hard for both when they are good friends. Dr. Yanover's facile conversational abilities had deserted him. His ready humor could not be called upon now. He spoke haltingly.

"I don't believe you can walk around for more than six months the way you are."

"No—no, Doc." My hands were shaking so hard I kept them down below the desk. "But—what happens next?"

"After that—life in a wheel chair." Dr. Yanover's kind eyes looked at me without pity—that would have meant the breaking point—but they were full of understanding.

I stared at the ends of my sleeves, at my clean white cuffs and the hands which I pressed together so hard my arms felt as though they were strung on wire.

"You can't mean that, Doc." My quavery words were like a child's defiance of the law of gravity, a swimmer's feeble struggle against an irresistible surf. Still I must fight. I could not stop. A life that was death waited.

"The family are depending on me—I can't become an invalid."

"Yes—I know," Dr. Yanover said. "Your mother is proud of you. She tells me you may be head of the Tax Department." He retained his professional tone but permitted a note of reassurance to enter his words. "There is a possibility—a slight possibility. I shall have to do some things—maybe it will turn out all right. What would you think of walking, really walking, on artificial limbs?"

This was more than I could stand. Doc had started out fair and square—then he had seen I couldn't take the truth. So now he was trying to soften it with vague promises of better things ahead. I could not answer him. I could not think. I could not feel. A numbness had gripped me like a steel trap.

But Dr. Yanover talked on quietly. And gradually some of the warmth and feeling of his personality crept into my heart.

"Don't give up, Hank. I have hope."

"What shall I do?"

"I want you to put yourself in my hands. Take a leave of absence from your job. Stop law school for a while—"

"I'm due to graduate in June."

"I *still* say—stop now."

"I've got to have time, Doc—this is a serious step."

Dr. Yanover's eyes were humorless as he said, "There's not much time."

Having to leave law school in the second half of your senior year may sound difficult, but such a decision seemed a trifle compared to the prospect of never being able to walk again. It is difficult, though, to hide your problem from those who are close to you. As the healthy color returned to Mamma's cheeks, her bright eyes took to scrutinizing me more closely. She seemed to sense the crisis I approached.

I walked out of school; it no longer seemed important.

I checked to be sure payments were made well in advance on my insurance policies—not that I was going to die, but there was a fatal feeling about what was happening.

I asked for a leave of absence from my job at HOLC.

And I said good-by to my friends at the office.

It was a casual announcement over a schooner of beer in a Ninth Avenue saloon near the McGraw-Hill Building. "I won't be in Monday."

"Anything wrong?" John Larkin said.

"I'm taking a leave of absence."

Ed Ford set his glass down on the cardboard coaster. "What's the trouble, Hank?"

"It's my legs. They're bothering me."

"Can we do anything?" John asked.

"No." I looked at the beer in my glass, which had gone flat. "It's something I'll have to work out by myself." Suddenly I felt cheap: that wasn't true. I would always have Doc.

Ed's eyes were puzzled. "Can Kay and I come and visit you?"

"No, I'd rather you didn't. But I'll see you sometime. Oh, come now, let's not make an Irish wake of this. Have another beer."

"Is Dr. Yanover helping you?" Mamma asked.

"He's giving me some treatments—to strengthen my legs," I said vaguely. "I'll be all right."

But it was only a surface assurance. The one thin slit of hope had been closed off. After a week of study and research into the old records on my case Dr. Yanover had jubilantly told me he was certain that I could wear artificial limbs, and had taken me to a designer of prosthetic appliances.

The limbmaker shook his head after examining me. "Nothing can be done."

"Never mind," Dr. Yanover assured me on the drive back to his office. "There are others."

"But he's one of the best, you said."

"There are others. And I believe it can be done."

But I did not dare to believe, and it was almost a physical feat on Dr. Yanover's part to get me to go to George Dorsch.

When I saw the gloomy shop under the Third Avenue El, with its anatomical window display, I shuddered. Alongside a false nose lay a collection of shiny steel splints, and a detached left hand wearing a wedding ring. Inside the shop a row of tall display cases along one wall bore crutches, braces, and artificial limbs in dusty array. It remined me of the waxworks at Coney Island, and I would not have been surprised to see Winston Churchill or Kaiser Wilhelm staring glassily out at me.

What I did see, however, once we were shown to the office, was a Prussian in the flesh in the person of George Dorsch, who snapped to his feet with an arrogance that belied his five-foot-two height and his little round belly.

Dorsch had a square gray mustache and he stared icily at us through his rimless glasses.

Dr. Yanover stiffened but his voice did not betray him. "This is my patient. Can you design a pair of limbs that will fit him?" He drew a sheath of sketches from his pocket. "I want something that will relieve the pressure here—" he pointed with a pencil—"and bring the weight to bear here— and here."

"Anyone would think, Dr. Yanover, that I do not know my business," Dorsch snapped. He turned his back on Doc, but his small eyes catalogued me rapidly. "Undress, please, and take off those boots. Sit over there." He pointed to an examination table on a raised platform out in the shop. "You may wait, Doctor, but it must be strictly understood at the outset that there will be no splitting of my fee. I shall deal only with the patient."

Dr. Yanover's cheeks flamed and he raised his head quickly. Then he clamped his teeth shut and strode away.

Dorsch marched into the shop with the assurance of a

ringmaster, and clapped his hands. *"Komm,* Fritz, Joe, Hans
—*schnell, macht schnell."*

Three or four healthy young men came on the double
with drawing pads and calipers.

The wheels were in motion and I was rolling willy-nilly
toward an uncertain destination. I turned to Doc for encouragement, but saw only his flushed face and angry eyes.
Then for a moment they softened into their accustomed
friendliness and he nodded reassuringly.

Dorsch seemed to be everywhere, though he remained in
one place, issuing commands to his corps of German youths
as they worked, and to me as I shifted my position from time
to time in an effort to follow his directions.

I looked up at the heavy beams and ponderous filigree of
the German gothic ceiling. It reminded me of a *Bier Stube*
I had once been in, yet something about it gave the impression of a church. Later I found out the place had served as
both.

In an effort to keep from thinking, I concentrated on some
white plaster casts which were hanging from one of the
heavy beams. But as I looked at them, a cold feeling like
trickling spring water inched down my back. On top were
the casts of the unbelievably deformed limbs of a small child.
I cannot hope . . . I will not hope, I kept repeating to myself.

"Jawohl," Dorsch said. "I think we can do it. We will
make the limbs of aluminum."

The young men were putting away their sketch pads and
measuring devices.

Dr. Yanover was rising from the chair to which he had
withdrawn after Dorsch's rebuff, but from which he had
watched the procedure intently.

"You will come to me tomorrow afternoon for the casts,"
Dorsch addressed me.

I could hardly rise from the table. I could not concentrate on what was being said.

When we were outside, Dr. Yanover took a deep breath, and waited for an elevated train to roar past. "This city air smells sweet."

"How could you stand his insults and his arrogance?"

"The man is a genius. He'll do it." Doc's words did not convey anything to me for a moment. Then he smiled, a smile that lighted up his entire face. "Don't you know what this *means*, Hank? You're going to have *legs*."

He took me back to Dorsch's the following day and after that I was on my own. But, distasteful as the atmosphere of the place must have been to him, he saw me through the first step, the making of the plaster casts.

I was shown into one of Dorsch's Spartan examining rooms. One of his young men put small cotton socks on my stumps and wrapped them in wet plaster bandages. When these had hardened he split the shells into halves and carefully removed them to make the molds.

In the weeks that followed I saw them form the metal "sockets" which were perfectly fitted to the contours of the plaster casts of my limbs; then the aluminum legs with knee joints that resembled more than anything else a jointed doll that once belonged to my sister Rose. Measurements, consultations, questions—still it was a dream. I would surely wake up. The question, "How tall will I be?" and Dr. Yanover's answer, "Not quite as tall as I, but almost," would be purely rhetorical. "We will make you five foot eight," Dorsch had said. I could not believe it. They were talking about somebody else. I was three foot eight. It was a game. And yet, could I hope?

Mamma's questions: "Is Dr. Yanover helping you? Is the pain going away? Why must you go into town so often?"

Stop it. *Stop it,* I wanted to say. The game has run over-time.

"Today we must decide about the feet," Dorsch said. "The feet must be made to fit the shoes instead of the other way around."

"Will they be of metal too?" I asked.

"No, they will be of willow wood. It is solid, sturdy, but lighter than metal. What size shoes would you prefer?"

I looked at Dorsch blankly. It was raining steadily outside and I had the feeling that any minute the wax ears and noses in the case would melt and run away, that Dorsch and the shop would disappear. What size shoe? It was Cinderella, the glass slipper, and all the fairy tales of my childhood drift-ing past in a gray stream.

How could I answer his question? I had no idea what sizes there were. I wished that Doc were here. He would have known.

"If you had lost your legs we would know the size you had worn, but since you never had any—" Dorsch shrugged. "We will make them size eight and a half. That ought to do. Come."

Out in the street he tried to hold his big umbrella so as to shield me from the downpour. It was so far above me that it did little good, but I did not care. I was fascinated watch-ing the shoes that splashed by, wondering which was eight and a half.

The shoestore smelled good, with the pungence of clean leather. The clerk seemed pleased to see customers on such a dreary afternoon.

"What size?"

"Eight and a half, C," Dorsch said.

A puddle was forming under Dorsch's umbrella, which leaned against a chair.

When the salesman returned, he started to remove Dorsch's shoe with the comment, "This may not fit you."

Dorsch waved impatiently. "They are not for me but for him."

The salesman looked at my leather-bound stumps. A shocked expression momentarily betrayed him.

"We will take them," Dorsch said.

That is how I chose my first pair of shoes, with no attention to the style. They were black with pointed toes, like the shoes that Dorsch wore. I never bought another pair like them. But they were magic shoes just the same.

I could not stay long with Mamma and the girls for fear I would tell them the secret. I could not stand being alone for fear of thinking. I could not bother Doc, he had other patients to see. What could I do? Suppose it didn't work? I must hold on to this thought. The other was too dangerous. Just remember this: You will at least have the limbs. Sitting in a wheel chair the pain will probably be gone and you will be as tall as other men. But do not dare to think you can walk among them. With a cane? No, not with a cane. With crutches? No, not even with crutches.

If only I had my work to do. The waiting was too much.

The day came.

The new legs were ready to be tried.

All the yearnings and anxiety could be fulfilled or abandoned. Mamma and the girls might be suspicious of what was transpiring, but at least none of my friends knew. I would be spared parading my disappointment before them if the experiment should fail.

I looked back at the house as I hobbled in the direction of the subway. I would never see it again—at least not as myself. The man who returned home would be a different person.

The ride was doubly tortuous. I wanted to turn back, but the rushing train impelled me toward my destination.

The shop was busy when I arrived. Dorsch bristled with suppressed excitement, though his voice was as usual. "The limbs will soon be finished," he said. "Come to the fitting room."

I sat on the cot, breathing hard, when one of Dorsch's men brought them in. The shiny legs looked very long. The checkstraps at the knees and the leather corsets looked efficient and complete. And on the feet were plain gray socks resembling those that Dorsch wore—and, my magic shoes.

"Thank you, Fritz. You may leave." Dorsch's matter-of-factness carried me through this moment.

When the workmen had left the shop and he and I were alone, he helped me put on the soft woolen stump socks that were made to fit my legs. While he worked, he talked quietly. He told me of his early life in Germany. He was more friendly now that he had ever been. This was the way Doc would have handled it. Dorsch told me how as a boy he had been apprenticed to a limbmaker. He mentioned quality. And he told me that the quality was not only in the limb, but in the man who wore it. These were the things Doc would say.

He carefully adjusted the waist straps and the lacings of the leather corsets that fitted around my stumps, and I sat looking at the strange knees as he adjusted a screw there. "At first we will make the tension tight. Afterward, when you have learned to control the bending of the knees, it may be loosened. Now, all is ready—but you have no trousers."

He went back to his office and returned with a pair of his own, which he carefully slid on over the limbs. They gapped at the waistband, but they cleared the shoes by four inches.

"Good, all is ready. Put your arm over my shoulder—there."

For a moment I had a feeling that Dorsch was a window

decorator and I was a dummy he was propping into position. Maybe I should be put inside one of the glass cases along the wall. With surprising strength the little gray-haired man propelled me toward the corner of the room where I braced myself, breathing hard. I felt as though I had climbed to the top of a tower and would plunge headlong at any minute.

"Hold this bar for balance," he said. "Now—"

He darted to the other end of the room and swung a full-length mirror around so that it caught my reflection head on.

I looked at a tall stranger, but the stranger had my face. A very white face.

This was the man who might have been born. It was a new man. A new life. This was the first day of it, the first hour, the first minute. As I looked it seemed as though this new life hung suspended precariously. But even if death should take me now, it would not matter. I had lived. If Doc had promised me nothing more than this moment it would have been enough for the lifetime of waiting.

I wept—uncontrollably, but unashamed.

Dorsch helped me to a chair, then scurried off and returned with a cold bottle of dark beer which he poured into two glasses. He held his glass up in salute. "This beer has quality," he said, but he looked away from me as he sipped it.

To be born is not enough. One must learn to walk.

There were intensive days of preparation. The dead weight that must be hoisted from the chair when I rose to my feet, and the muscles that must be trained to do it. The clumsy movements on crutches in Dorsch's shop as I swung my body forward from the shoulders, and dragged the unco-operative legs after me, while Dorsch counted time. The lifting, the panting, the complete exhaustion, and Dorsch's continued counting. The trailing of the unco-ordinated feet. What continually surprised me during these lessons was that I was taller than Dorsch. I felt as though I were some robot that he had created and was now trying to train for a well-mannered life. There were so many times when I would lose my balance and sway toward the wall, breathing hard as I hung in the crutches.

"It will come," Dorsch promised.

Sometimes I did not believe him, even though it did seem as if my swing were slowly becoming more smooth. And my legs did not bob in quite the detached way they had at the start.

Then we were ready for the first step without the crutches. Dorsch assisted me to my feet, and slipped two canes into my hands. I stood free and clear, with only the canes for support, and watched myself in the mirror.

Dorsch backed away. "Now, walk toward me." It was as though I stood on stilts, looking down at him. But specially contrived stilts—stilts that were hinged in the middle and would collapse suddenly if the delicate balance were disturbed. This was the real test.

And I couldn't move. I was frozen to my tottering supports.

"Come, come," Dorsch said. "Do not be afraid."

It was impossible. I could not move. I can do it, I can do it. *I will do it,* I told myself. But the muscles did not respond. I was slipping, slipping. My body sagged. I fell, and sat on the floor, with the long limbs protruding straight ahead of me, like an overgrown child. Tears of bitterness filled my throat and I threw the canes aside.

Coming quickly, Dorsch braced me against his shoulder and directed me to reach up to the bar. Then with an effort that cost every bit of my strength I raised myself to my feet.

"Rest a minute. Now—we will try again."

Fail and try. Fail and try. Try again. Again.

There was a moment when I knew I could not possibly

take a step. Then there was a moment when the leg was moving slowly, the knee flexing, sliding . . . sliding, balancing on nothing . . . my teeth clenched, my muscles taut with strain.

"Weight forward, use the canes—easy, easy," Dorsch said.

My weight shifted to the other foot.

"You have walked!"

Now they were tears of joy.

How often I was to think of that day in the shop, and to thank Dorsch for his relentless training, when in later years I helped wounded soldiers to take their first steps on artificial legs in the Maryland woods.

But Dorsch was not through teaching me yet. He supplemented the Prussian cadence of his walking lessons with training in how to drive. We took his car down near the East River on a street where there was little traffic.

Again Dorsch was explicit. "You will not be able to feel the foot pedals. You will have to listen to the sound of the motor to know how much you are accelerating. And when you are driving in traffic it will be hard to hear. But you will learn."

Dorsch was years ahead of his time. The new theories of physical medicine and rehabilitation were not yet widely known.

As the days progressed I found myself counting the hours, then the minutes, till I would be in Dorsch's shop, slipping into the new limbs and working with them. Reluctantly I put them off after each day's lesson, even though it was work and it was fatiguing. And always it was painful. Dr. Yanover had warned me that wearing the limbs would probably result in some changes in the contours of my own stumps, and that adjustments and manipulations would be necessary before they fitted comfortably. Old incisions opened and drained and new ones were irritated.

"The secret is in balance," Dorsch would say. "You must always anticipate a step or a rough part of the road. Remember you have less muscular adjustment to unusual conditions than a man with his own limbs."

Work. Work. Work.

One day he told me, "You are now ready to go home to your Mamma. You have learned to walk very well. Now you can drive a car; you have already thrown away one cane, soon you will use none at all."

A chill enveloped me. "Are you sure? I think I need more practice—"

"You are ready."

"But I have no clothes that fit." I was pleased at this inspiration. My specially trousered suits would not even reach to the knees of my new legs.

"You will wear my pants home." Dorsch dismissed the problem.

He drove me to Elmhurst that night, and left me at the door. "This is no place for me," he said. "If anyone, Dr. Yanover should be here. Perhaps it is best for you to go in alone. I will see you tomorrow."

I did not ring the bell, although the keyhole was so much farther down that I had to fumble for it. It had been chest high before.

The hall was dark. I could see a crack of light from the door to the kitchen, where Mamma and the girls were probably at supper. Our dog scampered toward me in the dark and barked. Then he sniffed. I could not feel him brushing against my legs but I knew he was there.

"I'll be right out," I called.

I wish that Doc could have stood with me in the doorway

and seen Mamma and the girls as they looked up from the kitchen table.

"The trousers don't fit," I said, "but they were the best I could borrow."

It broke the silence like a firecracker in church. And I crossed the threshold into a new life.

7

Love for Two Ladies

Mamma still sat quietly looking at me.

Dishes had been forgotten and the girls were taking turns parading me around the living room and comparing heights. I had it over sixteen-year-old Rose by a head and could better than hold my own with Terry, but Vicky was a bit taller than I.

"Stand up, Mamma—" I pulled her to her feet— "I can see the top of your head. Look, you just come to my chin." I felt like a giant, like a man wearing seven-league boots: I could do anything.

Mamma's eyes were swimming as she looked up at me. "It really is a miracle. St. Anthony's miracle."

"Don't you think Dr. Yanover should get credit for an assist?"

"St. Anthony wouldn't mind." Mamma smiled. "Tomorrow is Ash Wednesday. It will be almost like a birthday for you."

"How would you like to go shopping with me tomorrow after church?" I said. "Every mother ought to help pick out her son's first suit with long pants."

"What will you do with the old clothes?" Terry asked.

"Burn them," I said.

"How wonderful!"—this from Vicky.

It was the biggest and smelliest and most beautiful bonfire I had ever seen. The whole family was there in the back yard. Mamma quiet, but her eyes dancing as she fussed with the ties of her apron. Lil with a coat thrown over her shoulders; she had walked over from her house. Vicky helping me break up a cardboard box and stuff newspapers underneath. The fire got a good start, but then suddenly the old suits began to make a smudge. Rose dashed into the house and clattered down the basement stairs. She was back in a jiffy calling, "Here's the kerosene."

I doused a newspaper with kerosene.

"Stand back, everybody!"

I tossed it into the fire, which quickly flamed high.

"You forgot these—" Rose heaved a pair of work pants from the cellar into the middle of the blaze. Her cheeks were bright like those of a child who is doing something in defiance of rules but knows there will be no punishment.

Watching the smoke rush pungently skyward, I think Mamma and the girls shared my feelings. Because suddenly their laughter stopped. It was like destroying the remnants of an old and useless life.

It was so real to me that something that happened the following week seemed perfectly natural. I had stopped at the shoemaker's to pick up a pair of pumps belonging to Vicky. The man looked at me for a moment rather closely. "Say, what's happened to your brother—that little fellow who looked like you? He used to come in here once in a while."

"Oh, he's gone—he died." I was completely sincere. . . .

There is no thrill in life that can compare to that of walking up to a coin phone and putting a nickel in it—that is, when it has always been out of your reach before. There is nothing so joyous as to hold on to a strap on a subway train when up till now you have had to tilt your head back to even see the strap. Nothing so beautiful as the top of an automobile, if you have never been able to look over one before. I could lean on the mantel and wind the clock. I could see what was on top of shelves. I could almost touch the ceiling. I felt as though I were eight feet tall, taller than anybody else.

But not quite as tall as Dr. Yanover.

"I can't thank you. I can't ever repay you, Doc."

My voice wavered as I talked to him.

"I don't want to be thanked. Seeing you like this—" Doc cleared his throat— "it's a little more satisfying than taking out an appendix. I'll tell you what you can do, though. Some day maybe you'll have the chance to bring a new life to another boy. If you can help somebody else to feel the way you do today, that's all I'll ever ask."

"How can I do that, Doc? Nobody could possibly feel the way I do. I—"

Doc broke into a loud laugh. "You're really flying." But his voice was full of love and pride.

I certainly was flying. I was so busy steering my cloud around that I completely lost touch with the old life. Law school? I would never go back. Why study law when there were so many more important things to see and feel and touch? HOLC? Who wanted to be a tax expert? Life was waiting to be explored. But as my period of leave careened dizzily to its end, I knew I would have to return to my job.

By way of preparation I telephoned my boss, Tom Finn, and suggested that we meet Friday evening for cocktails. John Larkin was coming too.

At five thirty on Friday I entered the Longchamps at Broadway and Forty-first. . . . Good, they were at the bar. Working my way through the crowd in a wide arc, I came up behind them.

"Wonder what's keeping Hank?" John was saying.

I slipped up to the bar next to him and stood there unobserved for some time.

"How about another?" Tom said.

"Make that two, bartender."

"I'll have the same," I said.

John swung toward me. "Hi, Hank." Then he did a double take when he saw that I was not sitting on a bar stool.

Finn stared too. "What's in these martinis?"

"No D.T.'s. I'm real."

"Hank—" John took my arm—"it's wonderful. How did you do it?"

The smart-alecky reply that rushed to my lips hung there. John was crying.

"The next round's on me," Tom said. "Drink up, Hank."

"No, thanks," I said. "My doctor only allows one drink at a time. I have to balance myself on these things. You go ahead though."

A half-hour later I left my friends, slapping each other on the back and drinking chain-fashion, and took a cab to the Hudson River and the Jersey ferry. Ed and Kay had invited me out to their house for dinner. The ropy, tarry smell of the docks was fresher than usual that spring evening. How I loved it. I could hardly keep from singing, and shouting my good news to everybody I saw.

I picked out Ed, who towered over most of the crowd on the railroad platform at West Orange. Casually I walked toward him, though I did watch for the cracks between boards and any unsuspected step-downs. When I was near

Ed I brushed against him and gave him a slight push with my shoulder.

"What's the big idea?" He turned toward me, one arm shot back. "Why don't you watch where you're going?"

"Wanta fight?" I laughed. Ed's head jerked at the sound of my voice. "My God, it can't be—"

"Yes, it is." I slipped my free arm through his.

"It can't be true," he kept repeating, and he was still shooting confused questions at me when we drove up to his house. "Boy, will Kay be surprised."

Kay was. She opened the door, took one look at me, and fainted.

My cloud was really soaring. I was quite a guy—men wept, women fainted, life was exciting. I could do anything. I had to do everything.

The first day at the office I did very little work. Delegations from every department visited me all day. People whose names I hardly knew. People whose faces seemed fuzzy and not remembered . . . "We heard about you" . . . "Do you think your doctor could help my sister?" . . . "Gee, it's swell, Hank. How does it feel?" . . . "How does it feel?" . . . "How does it feel?" . . . "Gee it's swell . . . How does it feel?"

I remembered once, a long time before, seeing one of the stenographers typing away at a desk piled with presents. Over her head swayed a big wedding bell, trailing paper streamers that were tacked to the corners of her desk. Her friends had had a shower for her during lunch hour. That day I felt just as conspicuous and happy and important as an office bride.

At three o'clock Tom came over to my desk. "Why don't you take off, Hank. You're demoralizing the staff." He straightened his breast-pocket handkerchief and his eyes narrowed in a grin. I was glad to leave. And—I was beginning to feel tired. . . .

The new life brought problems too. Although I may have looked normal, I was still skittish about riding in the subway. I knew that even a slight disturbance of the delicate balance could send me into a sprawling fall. And once down, it was a real problem to get up again.

The rudimentary knee which I had always had on my right stump was most helpful in bringing muscle co-ordination to bear on my right limb, but the kneeless left stump created a considerable problem. (Even today I cannot maintain the same degree of control over the left limb as the right.) The most obvious result of this was that when I was sitting down, the left limb had a tendency to extend sideways. On the subway this sometimes resulted in another passenger's tripping over my protruding foot or being greatly inconvenienced. And I often found myself the object of stares and remarks, both unkind, directed not as formerly at a poor helpless cripple, but at a rather boorish individual with no regard for others.

However, I had so long schooled myself in the defense of staring back at the other passengers in the old days that I found myself still operating under the same rules. The results were not always good. If the victim was a man who happened to rest his eyes on me, he got a cool ocular dressing-down that sometimes led to his offering to settle the dispute on the platform at the next station, or if he was less aggressive, to his meekly returning to the pursuit of the colorful commentary on domestic life offered by his tabloid. If my adversary were female, the result of my insolence might be a homicidal glance, a coquettish nod, or a becoming blush.

Such incidental meetings with women made me realize there were other delights in this new life. I had attributed the attentions of the girls at the office to friendship, sympathy, whatever you want to call it. Now I was beginning to feel as pleasantly self-conscious and exploratory as a boy of fifteen.

I can realize now how lucky I was to be blessed with a houseful of sisters. Had I been, for example, one of the "seven Viscardi boys" I doubt if I ever would have learned to dance.

The day I threw away my second cane, Vicky got out a stack of records and fed them into the record player. Rose backed up the furniture along the living-room walls, and Mamma and Terry settled in a corner to watch.

"I'm not sure he should do it. What if he has an accident?" Terry said.

"Shhh." Mamma smiled and nodded her head in time to the music.

"Now," Vicky was saying, "put your right hand here, just above my waist, and hold my hand—like this. Now, listen to the music. At first, we'll just walk in time . . . one, two, *da*, de-da, da *da* . . ."

"You're doing it all wrong." Rose jumped up from the edge of the sofa. "In school they had us start by pushing a *chair* around." She was quite serious.

"Well, Hank's not going to push any chair around. He's going to push me around—and like it." Vicky shook her dark hair out of her eyes and laughed.

A chair would be the least of my worries, I thought, after pushing my pair of "stilts" around. In spite of my dim outlook, though, and the interruptions caused by the arrival of Rose's high school beau and Vicky's current young man from the department store where she worked, we did progress. Before the evening was over, Terry had gotten into the act with another set of suggestions, and we had Mamma doing the waltz. By the end of a week I felt so sure of myself that I was able to tease Mamma about the other step she did, which she called the "fox trot," but which resembled a stationary polka more than anything else. "You'll never get anywhere dancing in one place," I told her. Those nightly sessions were full of fun and music and activity.

"You'll soon be ready to solo," Vicky said.

How soon I did not realize.

One Saturday night I ambled down to Junction Boulevard to buy a Sunday paper. I was in no hurry. Though an occasional person stared at me, I had now had my limbs for about three months, the canes had been discarded entirely, and I was beginning to feel less like a curiosity and more as though I belonged in the crowd of people who did their late marketing or visited on the corners in the summer evening.

As I passed a poolroom a well-dressed young man sauntered out. There was a familiarity about the squareness of his shoulders and his relaxed assuredness. Of course. He had been a basketball player in high school.

"Pete Matula, I believe."

He looked down at me. "The face is familiar, but not—"

"That's the truest thing you ever said—Hank Viscardi."

I never ceased enjoying the shocked looks on people's faces, and Pete did not disappoint me.

"How in the—"

"Oh, I decided I wanted to be a basketball star, so I got a guy to build me a pair of legs."

"Let's have a beer," Pete said with the *savoir-faire* of a gangster indolently ordering up a case of champagne. "I've got half an hour before my date. When was the last time I saw you?"

"That game in Greenpoint. Remember?" Again I felt the pounding of the ceiling overhead as I took my shower after refereeing a church-league tournament, the year I graduated from high school. When I went upstairs to find Pete, he was sailing through the most intricate steps with the fancier women the gathering had to offer. Although Pete had not made any outstanding contribution to the intellectual advancement of the century, he had gotten through college on an athletic scholarship, and turned loose on the dance floor he was magic. He was magic with the women too.

"How'd you like to go to a dance, Hank?" he said, as we leaned on the bar in Grogan's. "Friday night. I'll meet you here. Don't worry about a date, I'll fix you up."

I confided in Vicky, who looked very pleased. "It will be good practice," she said. "Just don't get scared and tighten up. You can do it."

The dance was over in Manhattan in a hall on the east side, not far from the Waldorf. And it was such a dream world to me that it might as well have been the Starlight Roof.

"Wait here. I'll find Estelle."

Pete left me by the door and sauntered through the gracefully moving dancers to the refreshment stand on the opposite side. He wore more padding in his shoulders than I did, and his suit was cut narrower through the waist. The only similarity in our dress was the shoes; his had narrow pointed toes like the ones Dorsch had bought for me. The ceiling of crepe-paper streamers twirled in the vibrations from the four-piece orchestra, and from time to time the spotlight turned from red to green to blue. It was a new and exciting world.

"Here they are." Pete was back with two of the prettiest girls at the dance. Estelle was a platinum blonde, edged with mascara, and Bobbie was a redhead with legs like a Powers model. We watched Pete and Estelle take off. "I may see you later," he called.

"You a friend of his?" Bobbie said.

"Yes—basketball," I muttered vaguely.

"Can you do the Peabody?"

"What?"

"Aren't you going to dance?"

"Of course." I tried to make my voice sound authoritative. What in the world was the Peabody? If it was the series of swoops and dips Pete was executing, count me out. The only reason my knees were not shaking was the obvious one.

It was slaughter. I did all the things Vicky had warned against and forgot the things she had told me to do. Bobbie danced much closer than my sisters, and her clinging perfume nearly overpowered me. Through a stroke of luck we did wind up at the edge of the floor when the music stopped. I wanted to wipe my forehead but was afraid to take out my handkerchief. It would look awkward.

"Where do you come from—*Jersey?*" Bobbie said.

"No, I'm from Elmhurst."

"Really?"

Bobbie seemed to be peering through the crowd in all directions at once. "Say—uh, Hank, you don't mind, do you? A very good friend of mine has just come in. I have to tell her something. I'll see you later!" She patted my sleeve affectionately and left.

I relaxed and turned back to watch the crowd. No chaperones were in evidence, but I noticed a large neatly dressed man who kept circulating and seemed to be keeping things in order. Now and then Pete sailed by with an enraptured girl, his feet barely touching the floor. Once I saw him dancing with Bobbie. Then another girl came up to talk to me. Her name was Hester and she had beautiful eyes and a low-cut dress. "Don't yau wanta dance?"

"No, thank you." It was the tone Mamma had taught me when I visited around the neighborhood on 101st Street as a child. "I've already had one dance, and I don't believe I care to right now."

I was enchanted at being part of such a gay evening, and

I left early, feeling that I had tasted life. The last I saw of my friend Pete, he was off in a surge of motion, passing everything on the floor while the lights were turning green and purple.

The year passed, and it was March 2, 1938. Ash Wednesday. I took Mamma to church, then went to the office, where, after my routine work was finished, I wrote a long letter to Dr. Yanover:

This is Ash Wednesday, the first anniversary of a new life, and without you to celebrate, it would be empty, for it is the anniversary of your achievement. It was a year ago today that I recall tottering up the steps of St. Bartholomew's Church to receive the blessed ashes for the first time, and every act since then has been a new action in a new universe, for to me, life begins at that moment. . . .

For a time the intoxicating joy of living as a normal man has been so great that all ambition died too, and every hour was the exploration of a new world; nothing material existed, and even death would have been a mockery for the supreme pleasure of having lived only for an hour free of the stigma of deformity. . . .

This is for me truly the springtime of all life, of living. . . . I cannot live and reflect on each new experience without offering thanks to God and to you who have brought about this miracle.

You remember the boy who was, and now you know the man he became. Last night I was dancing. Can you believe that? And it was not myself who carried the rhythm, but you too; and so it will be in everything I do. I can never walk alone in this joy again, for every step I take is partly yours. No matter where I may be, you will always be with me, beside my bed at night, at my desk, and beside me when I walk.

How weak and useless are any words of mine to adequately express thanks to you for this? . . .

How useless indeed, but I finished the letter.

If any blessing springs from the grace of the Holy Ashes, it is my wish that it may be showered on you and yours, forever.

Doc would understand even if he had to remove the trim-mings from what I feared was a rather lavish display of words.

One summer, while I was still attending Fordham, I had spent a day at Setauket with some friends. While we were fishing for flounders in a rowboat, a fellow came by in a small sailboat. When he was fairly close, he came up into the wind. The tackle creaked while the sails flapped loosely, then slowly filled, and he was off on a new tack. As I watched, it occurred to me that it would be almost like riding on a cloud. I had always had a vague idea that I wanted to sail, even back in the days of Gouldie's paper boats. Now I was sure. It looked as though once you had your sails set you could sit back and relax and dream forever.

It was a while before my sailing progressed to that stage, but you have to start somewhere. I began with a square-stern sponson canoe, which I decided to build from the directions I found in a book. The book also had two chapters devoted to sailing it.

A high school teacher rented me his garage, which I con-verted into a workshop with the help of the tools and work-bench from Papa's old "laboratory." A neighborhood friend, Tony Jacovine, whom we called "A.F.," volunteered to help. This would be easy, I decided, and sailing it would be a dream. A sponson canoe is practically uncapsizable because of the air chambers which run its full length on either side. So we set to work. There were many setbacks, one of the worst caused by my decision to make the stern of ash. It sounded good. It was too good—I could hardly cut it, even with a chisel. However, as time passed, one of the biggest spurs to our finishing the job was the prodding of the high school teacher's wife, who had been only mildly interested in the project at the start and was now eager for us to be finished as soon as possible because of the hours her husband spent kibitzing in the garage. Spurred on by his attention, I developed an unjustified self-confidence. We fitted out the canoe with a mast, a leg o' mutton sail, and a bronze centerboard salvaged from an old wreck, and named her the *Eph Tutt*.

When the canoe was finished, A.F. helped me load its seeming ton of dead weight onto a borrowed truck and we toted it to Port Washington on Manhasset Bay. The launching was accomplished with a maximum of effort and we set out on the maiden voyage.

A.F. sat amidships and I shoved us off from the dock and perched aft on the only seat, by the tiller. I had the book open on my lap to the pages that gave the directions for sailing.

While I fussed with the rigging and gave A.F. directions for hoisting the sail, he began to complain, "This thing leaks."

I had noticed some time earlier that it was sprinkling, but had thought it best not to mention it. Now I said casually, "It's just the rain."

However, as we hoisted sail, and slipped out into the channel, it became apparent that a heavy downpour could not fill the canoe as rapidly as it seemed to be taking on water. Then I realized what had happened. I had had trouble making the rudder fit and had unscrewed the rudder gudgeons. It didn't matter as long as the boat was empty, but when A.F. and I got in, the gudgeon holes were way below the water line.

A.F. could not swim, and the sight of me calmly perusing the book on sailing did not add to his feeling of confidence. The climax of the trip came when a tug towing a string of garbage scows bore down on us tooting wildly. We were plumb across its course.

"Let out the sheet, let out the sheet!" I shouted to A.F., and began to paddle like mad for shore.

A.F. was a compliant crew on that trip, but once he set foot on the dock and wrung out his breeches, he vowed he would never sail with me again. He kept his promise.

As the years passed the *Eph Tutt* was succeeded by the *Eph Tutt II* and the *Eph Tutt III*, a small centerboard sloop which I built one winter at Port Washington. I decided to give her a Genoa jib, which was against all rules as this big, far-reaching sail was too much canvas for a boat of her size. Mamma helped me sew the sail at home, but she smilingly refused my invitation to come aboard. The Genoa jib lasted till the jib stay parted in a stiff breeze. After that we sewed up a working jib.

However, the boat had attracted the attention of a doctor, who offered to buy her. I was loath to part with my latest love which I had spent so many months creating, until he told me where I could get a twenty-two-foot racing sloop.

"It's too much boat for me," he said, "but I think you can handle her."

It would be a faster boat, I knew. . . .

So, I became the possessor of the *Eph Tutt IV*, a sleek fin-keel sloop, gaff rigged. The doctor then confided to me that he planned to sail his new boat to Huntington Harbor.

My jaw dropped. "That's close to sixty miles of open-water sailing from Port Washington, if you have to tack. I'd put it on a trailer if I were you, and haul it overland."

The doctor laughed at my suggestion. "Nope, gonna sail it home."

I knew he lacked experience; and I must confess that it was more from a reluctance to see the *Eph Tutt III* piled up on the rocks than from any concern for his welfare that I finally prevailed upon him to let me sail him there, and make delivery of the boat at Huntington.

We checked the weather and set forth at a quarter to five

one Saturday morning, despite the doctor's protest that it was the middle of the night. He came aboard wearing a fancy yachting cap and brand-new sneakers. I stowed the sandwiches and jug of water I had brought and we shoved off.

"My wife's going to wait dinner for us at Huntington," he confided, as we sailed out into Manhasset Bay headed for the Sound on a broad reach. I shook my head and made everything fast. As we sailed across almost all the way to New Rochelle, to clear Hempstead Harbor and avoid Execution Rocks, I sniffed the morning air.

"We've got a good day, Doctor."

"Mind if I stretch out and take a snooze?"

"Not at all."

It was not going to be a quick trip. We did not have exactly a following wind, but it was suitable for reaching and it looked as though it would hold.

The weather did hold. The sun was bright, clear, and hot. We tacked repeatedly. By four P.M. when we rounded Lloyd Neck at the entrance to Huntington Harbor, the doctor was stretched out again, this time in the bilge, where he huddled retching, with his shirt sleeves pulled down against the merciless sun and his yachting cap askew.

For the first time it occurred to me to wonder if he had ever been on board a sailboat before. We were running a foul tide and I knew we would have trouble sneaking into the harbor. With every creak of the mast and sway of the deck, the doctor groaned.

"Let's beach the boat," he said. "There's land."

"And walk five miles through the woods? Not on your life."

"I beg you—"

"No, sir. You engaged me to sail this boat to Huntington and that's where I'm taking her."

A wave of nausea temporarily quieted the doctor.

The moon was up and the Coast Guard were out looking for us when we reached the anchorage. Dinner was waiting —everything from fruit cup to strawberry shortcake, with large portions of roast beef in between. I ate dinner, then started in on the fruit cup again and went right through the second time. The doctor wasn't hungry.

After the Incident of the Seasick Doctor, the Sound was my oyster. On week ends I sailed its length and breadth, exploring the fashionable coves and the mud flats. I got to know the tides and currents like a brother; I found out where the tom cods lived and I knew the best time and place to troll for striped bass. And my constant companion, my love, a lady named *Eph Tutt*.

As I sailed her up the Connecticut rivers and visited the noisy shipyards, or relaxed in the cockpit in the warmth of the sun's rays, the portable radio reminded me that the world was at war. One after another, the European countries had bowed to a new aggression. But Europe was a distant world. My world of soothing breezes, of mischievous currents, and strong but predictable tides was at peace.

One fall morning I pumped the bilge, and set out from Manhasset Bay for my usual Saturday sail. From the looks of the sky it might only last a couple of hours. I reflected that if it had been brighter I might have persuaded Vicky and Rose to come along. None of the girls had ever sailed with me, but they always seemed to be on the point of yielding.

I stowed my oilskins in the forward locker, hoisted the sails, and cast off. The breeze was puffy, but outside the shelter of the headland it picked up and I headed toward clear water. As I trimmed the mainsail and jib, I saw another sloop manned by two girls inching up on the port quarter. They were gaining rapidly and soon came abeam. They waved. So, they wanted to race, did they? All right, I'd show them. Reaching for the sheet, I close-hauled the mainsail and trimmed the jib to a knife edge. The *Eph Tutt's* long overhanging boom and high-peaked gaff packed plenty of square yards of canvas between them. We shot ahead, just in the nick of time, for the other sloop was about to steal our wind.

As we raced out into the Sound I realized the wind was freshening. My bare arms were covered with gooseflesh, but I didn't want to take the trouble to slide forward to the locker for a sweater. Since I could not kneel, and hoisting myself to my feet in a pitching boat was difficult, I had learned to stay put when under sail.

A whoosh of spray soaked me as we spun on. I looked at the sky, which had suddenly turned to lead. As I watched, the mainsail slackened and the tackle began to groan. The girls in the sloop had passed me and were coasting merrily through the white-capped waves.

Steal my wind, would they? I knew my boat was faster, so I decided to tack and sneak up on their port side. The *Eph Tutt* sheared into the sea, but it was a rough tack. We were taking a lot of spray and the boat worked with the strain. The wind was rising rapidly.

This is a squall. I'd better head for shore, I thought. What were those crazy girls doing? They had tacked, too, and if I could judge were taking plenty of back talk from the waves. I shifted my position and realized I was sitting in a pair of sopping wet dungarees. I slacked off the sheets to shorten sail, and we pitched as the growing waves shoved under the *Eph Tutt's* bow.

Just then I saw the sail of the sloop swing over toward the water, but she didn't right herself. I jerked the tiller, ducked the boom, and came about. They had capsized.

When I reached the sloop, I could see the girls in the water holding to the edges of the wet sail. I threw a line to the closest one and her companion was pulled aboard a cruiser which had come up from the other side. I saw that the cruiser was fastening a towline to the sloop, as I landed my soaked but attractive catch.

"Are you all right?"

Her hair was pasted to her neck in soaking ringlets. She smiled and nodded her head as she crawled into the cockpit.

"You'll find a sweater and some oilskins in that locker, and maybe a towel."

While she dried herself and bundled up in my clothes, I headed for shore. The wind slacked off and the sun came out before I got her back to the yacht club. Her hair was beginning to pick up glints as she rubbed it with the towel.

"Lucky you came along," she said.

"If I hadn't, maybe you wouldn't have gotten into trouble."

She laughed. "Sometimes it's fun to get into trouble."

Her name was Betty and she was easy to talk to. A good sailor, too, as I learned on the few trips we had together on the *Eph Tutt* before the season ended. I even invited her to have dinner in town, and scarcely realized till afterward that Betty had been my first actual date. It all seemed so natural. But with the waning of the sailing season I saw less of her. During the winter I spent all my free time up at Noroton, Connecticut, where I was building a ketch in a boat yard on the Five Mile River, and by the following spring I had discovered a very attractive girl.

Elaine was fresh from college and looked upon her clerical job as the start of a career. She still wore her hair long like a schoolgirl's and would have looked more at home writing an examination in "Economics 1" than compiling figures that might add up to the failure or success of a man's lifetime ambition.

"How do you spend your evenings—reading magazines that tell how the young business girl should dress?"

Elaine's eyes were wide. "You're teasing me."

"I'm not really, but it might be fun to. Why don't you have dinner with me some night?"

It was fun. We went to a French place up in the sixties. Elaine hung on my words and deferred to my judgment in everything. When I asked her what kind of wine she would have with the duck-in-orange-sauce she looked at me trustingly and said, "You decide."

Suddenly I felt an overpowering urge to protect this girl. When she asked me to talk about myself, her simplicity was so disarming that I cast off the role of man-of-the-world which I had assumed at the office. It didn't seem cricket to deceive her.

When the crêpes Suzette had stopped flaming and we were about to put our forks into this brandied delight, I looked at Elaine seriously. "I'd like to tell you a story. . . ."

I went back to the little boy at the hospital and by the time I had gotten to Dorsch and the limbs we were sipping small glasses of Benedictine.

Elaine's eyes were larger than I had ever seen them and her eyelids were brimming. "What did your mother say when you walked into the house that first night?"

"Mamma said, 'It's a miracle.' "

Elaine dabbed at her eyes with her napkin. "I—I—oh, Hank, excuse me."

She fled from the table in the direction of the ladies' room.

I sipped the last of my Benedictine. Elaine's unfinished glass sat at her empty place.

"Another Benedictine?" the waiter said.

"No, make it brandy."

"Will that be all, sir?"

What had happened to Elaine? I went out and spoke to

the checkroom girl. "I'm afraid the young lady I'm with may be ill."

The waiter had removed his change tray from the table when Elaine returned.

"Don't get up—please," she said. There were suspicious streaks of powder on her cheeks and her eyelids were rimmed with red.

"I didn't mean to make you cry. Will you finish your cordial?"

She shook her head. The look in her eyes made me feel slightly giddy and very important. Outside, she tucked her small hand through my arm and I reached down and held it as we walked under the El in the warm evening.

On the train to her home, I talked to Elaine about sailing.

"You'll have to come out on my new boat."

"Does it have a name?" Her voice sounded sleepy.

"Of course. The *Eph Tutt*." For a minute I wondered how the ketch would look with *Elaine* stenciled on the transom.

"How big is it?"

I told her it was twenty-four feet over-all, with a cabin that would sleep two.

Elaine raised her head from the hollow of my arm. "With windows?"

"Portholes," I corrected.

"I could make curtains for it."

When I left Elaine at her house, her eyes told me more than her words—"It's been wonderful."

I kissed her on the forehead. "Good night, little girl. Don't forget those curtains you're going to make."

It was a long walk back to the railroad—but I was flying.

The ketch was up on her cradle in the shipyard. The portable radio was perched on the stern deck, and we were listening to the Sunday afternoon symphony. Elaine sat on one of the bunks in the cabin, wearing a checked wool shirt of mine that nearly covered her crossed legs. She held a heavy mug of coffee in both hands and sipped from it as she listened to me outline plans for rearranging the cabin.

"I didn't like that cramped galley we had last summer," I was saying. "By moving this locker, and sliding the bunk back to here, we can get two more feet of work space. Let's see, this is the first week end in December. By the midlde of January—"

The music on the radio stopped. "We interrupt this broadcast to bring you a special news bulletin. The Japanese Air Force and Navy have just attacked Pearl Harbor . . ."

A warm stickiness enveloped me. I wanted to blurt out, "We are at war," but instead I self-consciously twirled the dial in search of other news, maybe a contradictory report. But as we picked up the words that told of bombings, of submarine attacks, of battleships damaged and sunk, cruisers and destroyers melted to scrap, flames rushing skyward— Elaine's eyes grew rounder and her face whiter, and I finally looked at her and said, "It's serious. We should have seen it coming. There won't be any more sailing on this ketch. I've got to help."

I took a scrap of wood from the deck and with my pencil cut in a "For Sale" sign. Then I carefully wired it to the transom.

"And I never got the curtains made," Elaine said.

"Take a good look at her, Elaine." I helped her down the ladder to the ground. "You may never see this boat again."

Elaine threw both her arms around my neck and pulled my face down close to hers. She seemed so little and so unwilling to be touched by what had happened.

"Aren't you rushing into this?" she said. "Maybe it isn't so serious as you think."

8

Fort Dix

A world of khaki, of brown buildings and mud streets, of reveille and rifle range and week-end passes. Of moody patients at the station hospital. Of barracks-bag soldiers with their pregnant brides. Of privates changing tires on a major's convertible. Of outfits awaiting shipment. Of gold-brickers and PX wrist watches and courses in Military Protocol. And men.

I was part of it and proud.

But the road to Fort Dix had been rutty and full of detours.

There was the sunny detour of Elaine—with cool woods and a brook and meadowlarks. "Wait and see," she said. "Besides, they won't take you for military service. Don't go away."

There was the efficient parkway her father tried to direct me to, as he turned the knob on his humidor and offered me an after-dinner cigar. "Let me get you into a war plant. When this thing's over you'll have a nice little nest egg. I know—I came up the hard way."

There was the big fork where the route of Mamma and

122

the girls branched off. The road looked fairly even, but there were patches of shade and I knew there would be unsuspected turns ahead.

"Why must you go?" Mamma's dry eyes were harder to look into than a pool of tears. "You are the only man in the family. We will miss you."

"It isn't for myself," I said, "but I have a feeling I'll be needed. There is something I can do better than anyone else. I think I can help wounded men."

"You mean men who—lose their legs?"

I nodded.

"But how will you do that?"

"I don't know—Hospital Corps maybe. If that doesn't work, there's the Navy. I know a lot about handling boats."

"You must decide," Mamma said, "but I wish—"

There was the detour of the recently widened highway that belonged to the Marine Corps, over which platoons marched with perfection and amphibious vehicles rolled. The sergeant returned my papers smartly. "Sorry, you can't pass the medical exam."

There was the marble pavement that led into the Air Cadet Training School, but the gilt-lettered sign between the hedges could be seen from the road: "Only the Flower of American Manhood Need Apply."

Then I came to a wide river. A long line of traffic was waiting to go aboard the Coast Guard training ship anchored there. "Not a chance today," the recruiting yeoman said. "I doubt if you'd get a waiver on your physical disability anyway. Try the Navy if you want to, but their answer will be the same."

The answer everywhere was the same. Nobody wanted a cripple, not even the man-hungry Army, despite the rather tiresome anecdotes that were circulated all through the war about the draft board in Utah that sent a man with a wooden leg to an induction center five times to fill their quota, or the doctor who said, "Put this one in the Infantry—he's breathing." Every window was slammed in my face. It was one of those standard jokes that make a good newspaper story: MAN WITHOUT LEGS WANTS TO BE SOLDIER.

But I knew I had logic on my side: I could walk miles. I could build boats and sail them. I could help amputees learn to walk again. Able-bodied men would be drafted to pound typewriters and answer telephones, while I remained at home with the women and children—and even the women were going into service. Years later, when I became a personnel man, I was to learn that the concepts of ability set up by military and industrial organizations often have no relation to the physical demands of the job to be done.

However, there was one road I had not tried. I was guided to it by an Army doctor who had listened patiently to my story. "Have you talked to the Red Cross? I think that's the place for you."

The Red Cross interviewer shook his head.

"We can't give you a job doing physical therapy with amputees. That requires skill and special training—" he ignored my startled expression—"but we might possibly use you in our Field Service. You'd be attached to a military unit on active duty." He handed me a bunch of forms and I started in once more to encode my hopes, my ambitions, and my desires.

There was the evening in the spring of 1943 when I telephoned Elaine. "The most wonderful news. The Red Cross came through. The letter was here when I got home from work. I have until May 17th. I report to Washington."

I was so elated with the thought of getting into the service, of having the assimilated rank and pay of an Army captain, so flurried with plans for winding up my personal affairs, getting my work at the office in shape to leave, and writing notes to friends, that I gave little thought to how Elaine was taking it.

Her good-by was tearful, and I was half comforting but half dizzy with anticipation. "I'll be back before you know it." Then, with the derring-do of an H. G. Wells hero boarding the ramp of a rocket to the moon, I entered the train gate at Pennsylvania Station.

I had had a physical examination at the Army Induction Center in New York. This was followed by three weeks, at the national headquarters in Washington, of Red Cross indoctrination. It consisted mostly of facing the battery of shots inflicted on military personnel, and learning to live out of a foot locker and sleep on a cot in a former rooming house—now converted to a barracks and jealously kept by its owner, a woman who claimed to be a direct descendant of an Indian chief. Along with the professional men and school teachers from the Middle West who had joined the Field Service, I was issued Army uniforms, on which the Red Cross insignia were placed, and chits to be exchanged for required gear at an Army Quartermaster's store downtown.

At Fort Dix we were assigned to a basic training unit. We learned to shoot on the rifle range, we bivouacked with the troops, and we studied military procedures. We even marched under the direction of a drill sergeant, though I must admit he was a very kindly one, an actor from the legitimate stage who could only claim to be a *former* sergeant. After a medical discharge he had gone back into the service as a Red Cross field director. His name was Leo Henning.

One day Leo and I waited on one of the usual lines we had been standing in for weeks. The prize at the end of the line was something special—a pair of Army field boots. The man who would fit us to the wrong size was a very nice Army sergeant who spoke only in words of one syllable—and four letters. With the perversity born of dust, sweat, and sun, Leo and I decided to keep my artificial limbs a secret. So, as nonchalantly as possible, we removed our shoes and mounted the platform where the sergeant was engaged in his orthopedic fittings. His procedure consisted of measuring your ankle with one hand and shoving a pair of boots from a counter at you with the other, and telling you what you could do with them.

My turn came. The sergeant clutched my ankle. His hand froze there and an annoyed look clouded his maroon features.

"You'll have to let go," I complained. "It hurts."

"What in the ---- ---- ---- ---- ----?" With savage intent he rushed my other ankle. Then he really cussed. I have never seen such frustration. He hurled a pair of boots down in front of me.

"Christ," he commented, "at last the GI's answer to the meat grinder. These things won't even blister you."

I was the only man in the military forces who did not complain about "meat grinders"—GI boots.

At the Red Cross building, where we reported daily for indoctrination, part of our duties consisted of studying the procedures of chaplains and working with Red Cross field directors who were attached to activated regiments.

We interviewed patients at the station hospital, stateside casualties who were often bitter because they had been wounded without ever seeing combat. We had to chart the problems of the prisoners. These "barracks-bag" soldiers followed a pattern. They were drafted by the Army. They went AWOL. Or maybe they stole a car or got into a fancy crap game on furlough, or slept on guard duty—they were in trouble. They were put in the stockade. Their CO's got them transferred to another outfit where they started in all over

again. Sometimes there was a girl who accused the prisoner
of fathering her unborn child. Our job was easy: All we had
to do was convince him that he must marry her or get shipped
at once to a line outfit overseas. The Army never seemed to
solve the problems of these men; it just moved them around.

I was also becoming indoctrinated in the landscaped recreation provided at the Officers' Club. Seeing Red Cross girls
and Army nurses there in uniform, I suddenly missed Elaine
—Elaine in a ruffly blouse that had no lieutenant's bars, and
silly pumps that would have been as bewildered as she on a
drill field; Elaine whose correctly spelled letters were bub-
bling with laughter. It would be wonderful to see her walking toward me in the sunshine, to hold her in my arms—just
to be alone with her.

One Sunday near the end of my training period she came
down for the day. Everything was as perfect as I had planned
—from Elaine's flowered dress and white sailor hat to the
frosty daiquiri we sipped on the porch of the OC, and the
broiled chicken and green salad and architectural meringue
that followed. I wore my tailored summer uniform and had
polished my insignia almost down to the lead fillings. For an
hour or two it was as though we were dining at a Long Island
country club.

Her eyes were luminous when she said, "I've missed you,"
and I was thumping with pride afterward when I showed her
the club and the Red Cross building and took her for a walk
down the company street.

"Are you happy?" Elaine asked me. "You look wonderful.
. . . I like your uniform."

When it was time to take her to the train we could not get
a cab. I was worried about Elaine's sheer dress because the
sky was clouding over. Luckily the Fort Dix bus was at the
gate, and we climbed aboard. The interior smelled of dusty
leather. A sudden gust and a clatter of thunder, and the rain

poured down. Elaine, sitting next to me, looked like a child who had just been awakened from a beautiful dream.

"Oh, Hank—what's going to happen to us?"

I put my arm around her shoulder and looked deep into her teary eyes. "The U.S. Army and the Red Cross will see that everything is all right."

But she shivered.

When we reached the station at Trenton the sun was out again. "See, dear, you're not even damp. That's a pretty out-fit. . . . That's it—smile!" I kissed her good-by as the brake-man shouted, *"Board!"* and tossed her a jaunty salute just before her little white hat disappeared into the railroad car.

The next day I learned that we might get orders any time. I wondered if I would have a chance to phone Elaine before shipping out.

On Tuesday I got a call from a friend of mine who was working in Public Relations at the post—Sergeant Bob White.

"What do you know, Bob? Get some dope on my orders?"

"Nothing so dull as that. I want you to meet a friend of mine. Can I bring him around?"

In five minutes Bob was at my desk in the Red Cross build-ing with a tall, urbane-looking man in a white Palm Beach suit. He was prematurely gray at the temples.

"Hank, I'd like you to know Tom Slater. He has the radio show 'This Is Fort Dix.' "

"I've heard about you," I said.

"Could you come on the show Sunday?" Tom asked.

"Who—*me?*" I mugged it.

He nodded.

"I'm sorry, I'm waiting for orders, and I may not be here that long."

"Don't worry," Bob said, "we can probably arrange to delay you till after the broadcast."

"A soft life, this public relations—you guys know all the

angles." I turned to Slater. "I don't know why I should be on a radio show. I'm not sure I want to."

Tom made a joke to cover his surprise. Apparently he was not accustomed to being turned down.

"What do you do on the program?"

"Oh—interview men here at Fort Dix. Give the folks at home a little local color. Try to put on interesting personalities."

"I'll be frank, Tom. I entered the service for a purpose. And I don't see how being on a radio show can further that purpose."

Tom seemed interested, so while Bob chatted with a Red Cross girl at a nearby desk, I unburdened myself to him. I explained that I did not want to see Paris or Vienna or Berlin. I did not want to hold men's hands like a chaplain or persuade them to marry women they had gotten into a jam. I only wanted to get to a spot where I could help amputees readjust to living again.

"Hank, I just might be able to help. Let me talk to Colonel Turnbull."

Colonel Turnbull was the officer in charge of the station hospital. When I tried to salute him, he said, "We don't need any of that stuff—sit down." He was a real chicken colonel with a bird on his shoulder. I liked the way he came to the point.

"I've sent for you because Tom Slater's story interested me." His eyes were candid. "Yes—I could use you right here, son. We get plenty of station casualties—amputations even. But they'll need you a lot worse at Walter Reed. I'll write you a letter to take to General Marietta."

"Colonel," I said, "I appreciate your taking an interest in me, but it may be too late. I'm waiting for orders now."

Colonel Turnbull smiled with the assurance of military

authority. He pressed a button and a captain entered the room.

"We'll start the machinery going right now. You'll get orders, son, but you're not going far. Whatever happens, remember this: Just sit tight and wait till you hear from me."

9

March . . . March . . . March

I ordered breakfast from the printed menu in the Officers'
Mess at Walter Reed Hospital, noting that you could have
your muffins with or without blueberries, and passed up
both for the hotcakes. While I waited I started to write
today's letter to Elaine. There would be no time once I got
to my desk.

Darling,
    I can't tell you how much I've missed you since that last leave.
It's too bad I sold the *Eph Tutt*. We could have had a sail, but
just being with you . . .

Memories of our enchanted hours together rushed over
me. Everything about Elaine—a silly detail like the turn of
a nose, the spontaneity of a giggle from her corner of the
porch glider—was special and remembered, to be lingered
over thoughtfully and warmly. For the first time now I felt
that she was sure. I had been sure long ago.

    . . . I haven't gotten your answer on the dance yet—I hope you
can come . . .

Elaine would want to hear about Jerry. He was so important to me that I wanted to share the story with her.

Jerry's going home today, and Jerry is going to be all right . . .

"Mornin', Mr. V."

A pleasant drawl at my elbow and I looked into the eyes of the Red Cross recreation worker from Virginia. She seemed to be part of the sunny morning. "Anything new on the amputees' dance?" she said.

"The boys are rehearsing an orchestra up in Ward Sixty-four."

"How does it sound?"

"None of the other patients have succumbed—and they still have a week to practice. I think the Red Cross had you in mind when they designed that uniform."

"Go on now. What you aiming to ask for?"

"Since you inquire—be sure and put the General on the invitation list. He's dying to come."

"Will do." She hummed away.

I was glad that the General's blessing had finally put the details of the dance into the works. Getting permission from the Red Cross had been the hard part.

"A dance for enlisted men in the Red Cross building? Mr. Viscardi, it's never been done before. How can amputees dance? Some of the men don't even have uniforms."

I could see that no self-respecting male whose gear was still in Tunisia would want to attend a dance in the maroon pajama-like "fatigues" that were worn on the post.

"Issue them new ones. They'll need them eventually."

"It's impossible—"

"But think what it would do for their morale."

Yes, getting permission for the dance had been even harder than being assigned here. This was where I belonged, though. This was where sixteen Hank Viscardis belonged.

Colonel Turnbull had kept his promise. From Fort Dix I got orders down the Jersey shore to an activated Air Force unit awaiting shipment. The long arm of the military had pulled me out of there miraculously just before the squadron took off for overseas, and deposited me in Washington on the doorstep of Brigadier General Shelley U. Marietta, commanding officer of the Walter Reed Army Hospital, which then housed the only military amputation center in the country.

"I could certainly use you," General Marietta said. "I need you as badly as I need surgeons. I've got hundreds of amputees and thousands more coming. It would be an inspiration to them just to have a man like you around—even if you didn't do a thing."

The Red Cross acceded to General Marietta's request, and one morning a worker in the Military Liaison Section drove me out to the hospital and introduced me to Miss Margaret Lower, the kindly white-haired Red Cross director there.

It had been accomplished in six weeks from the day at Fort Dix when I first met Colonel Turnbull, but the waiting had seemed much longer.

Elaine's letter rested unfinished in my pocket when I left the Officers' Mess and walked to the Red Cross building. There was a note on my desk to call Miss Lower, the director.

"Mr. Viscardi," she said, "I'm very concerned. It must have slipped your mind. I have been advised that you have not turned in your reports. The area office is asking for them."

I liked Miss Lower's kind sympathy as much as I disliked writing reports. I thanked her for reminding me.

Over at the other desk, Thomas Blanford, the Red Cross official whose office I shared, nodded sadly. "Hank, I've warned you. You'll have to make case histories."

"Look, Tom, if I stop to write case histories, who's going to do my work? I can't even begin to see all the men who ask for me. And you know how late I stay every night."

Case histories— How would you write a case history on Bill, for example? With the military and clinical jargon skimmed off it would boil down to something like this:

Cpl. William ————, age 20, had a surgical amputation of the left leg below the knee, following loss of this extremity due to shellfire in Tunisia. He was a co-operative patient until he began to complain that the Army delayed in supplying him with an artificial limb. After the orthopedic surgeon in charge of his case had said he was ready to be fitted to a prosthesis, he was required to wait for six additional weeks, due to the heavy demands being made on the hospital shop for orthopedic appliances. At the beginning of the third week he addressed insulting language to an Army physician, a major, and used profanity in the presence of a first lieutenant of the Army Nurse Corps. Also, he became intoxicated as the result of drinking liquor which had been brought to him by a friend in violation of Army regulations. He was given a reprimand and ten days' confinement to a disciplinary ward where he became more abusive and unmanageable than ever. This behavior persisted for two weeks in spite of efforts of various staff members who visited him, including a psychiatrist. . . .

How would you put into the correct terminology the joy with which Bill responded when he was finally fitted to his limb? Even though it was only the poorly made temporary limb that the Army supplied, and on which he must struggle to walk until he was discharged and could get a properly fitted appliance from the Veterans Administration. My pride as he learned to balance himself during my unofficial lessons in walking certainly did not belong in the case history. And how would you set down the facts concerning the girl from his home state who worked at the Bureau of Ships and came to see him every Sunday, and with whom he planned to have his first date? The grace of her walk and the way Bill's young face lighted up when she entered the ward were not the sort of thing that you included in a case history. Neither would the area office want to hear about the steak she had bought with saved-up ration points and the arrangements she made for her three roommates to be away the first evening Bill would be allowed off the post.

What kind of report could capture the glow in his eyes as he limped down the steps of the Administration Building with two corpsmen, to be helped into a waiting cab? How would you describe the way he suddenly staggered at the last step—the splitting sound—and Bill lying there with the splintered half of his leg on the curb beside him, still wearing its GI shoe and sock?

His comment could not go into the report, of course. He had said, "God-damned matchstick!" while the corpsmen gently carried him back to the ward. He was still cursing bitterly when I visited him four hours later at the end of my evening rounds.

Another case that would defy the chronicler's efforts was that of the suicidal major.

We had had a long day. A convoy of wounded had been shipped in. As it was one thirty when I finished work, I bedded down in the chaplains' quarters. It seemed easier than going home to my room in a private house off the post, since I knew I should have to be up before seven.

At three o'clock the telephone beside my bed rang. It was one of the Protestant chaplains. "I hate to disturb you, Hank, but it's very important. Could you come over to Ward G-5 as soon as possible?"

I slipped into my limbs and put on my uniform.

Chaplain Barclay was waiting for me at the entrance to G-5, an officers' ward of private and semi-private rooms.

"Thanks for coming. We've got a real problem."

I waited.

"Do you remember a Major Cummings in that convoy this afternoon? He had lost his leg in a jeep accident in Hawaii."

"Yes."

"He's almost in a state of hysteria. Resents the Army and anybody who tries to help him. The orderly tells me he may be armed, though I don't see how, and that he has threatened to kill the first man who enters that door. I've tried to talk to him, but—"

Barclay was no alarmist, so I realized someone must get to the major.

"Do you want me to go in?" I asked.

"I can't ask that of you, but I thought if you already knew him he might listen to you."

"I didn't get a chance to talk to him today, but let me give it a try."

I knocked on the door and stepped into the room.

"I ought to blow your brains out," a voice from the bed greeted me.

"I'm an amputee," I explained, "so don't aim too low. It costs money to keep these things in repair."

"You're not funny." There was a long pause. Then he asked, "Which leg?"

"Both. Mind if I sit down?"

"All right, but lock the door behind you."

We talked for a long time. He was worried about how the loss of his leg would affect his insurance business. But his biggest concern was how his wife and twelve-year-old daughter would feel about having a one-legged man limp home.

"If they really love you, it won't matter." Then I showed him Elaine's picture. "This is the girl who loves me."

"She's pretty," the major said.

It was almost daylight when I came out into the corridor. The orderly was sleeping on a straight chair, but Chaplain Barclay's eyes were open.

"The major's asleep," I said. "Here are the letters he had written to his family. I promised to destroy them. Do you suppose you could use your ecclesiastical influence on the mess sergeant to get us some breakfast?"

"By the way," he inquired as we walked toward the Officers' Mess, "was he armed?"

I stopped on the path. "I don't know. I forgot to ask him."

I suppose the major's case would be handled in a few lines:

Major Cummings, 41 [then a terse summary of the medical findings to date], after admission to Walter Reed Hospital threatened to shoot a number of staff members, including this worker. He also threatened to commit suicide and in a three-hour interview we prevailed upon him not to do so.

My neck ached and my stumps were cramped, but I was only a tenth of the way through my mail, consisting of letters from the families of patients, when a Red Cross worker stuck her head in the door. "Mrs. McGee is here."

"Good. I'll see her outside."

In a corner of the lounge I talked to the pleasant Irishwoman who was the mother of Jimmy McGee. She spoke with just the taint of a brogue as she explained to me that Jimmy was her only child and how close they had become since the death of her husband several years before.

"I understand Jimmy's injury, and I think he does too—you've been with him to help his thinking." She was referring to Jimmy's loss—his right leg blown off by a land mine at Kasserine Pass. "But how about his friends, and his girl, Mr. Viscardi? That's so important to a boy. I know it would worry me a lot if I was in his place."

"Jimmy has a good attitude. I think he will be able to face those problems when the time comes."

There had been such a change in Jimmy since he was first admitted to the amputation center. Father Antonine Barrett, one of the chaplains, had asked me to go over and see him at the air base in Maryland. He was sullen at first.

"Did he tell you that he served Father Barrett's Mass this week?" I said.

"Yes." Her face glowed.

"The only complaint was that he could not kneel with the artificial leg. He claims we have given him a Protestant leg and he wants it changed."

We both laughed.

I said good-by to Mrs. McGee a trifle reluctantly. It was time for my next appointment. I had to break the news to a father that his son had lost a leg.

When I got back to my office just before lunch, Rabbi Neumann stuck his head in the door. He grinned broadly and tossed me an exaggerated salute. "How about doing me a favor, Hank?" Then he told me about the boy he'd seen that morning at the Walter Reed amputation annex out at Forest Glen. The chaplain shook his head. "It's a difficult case. He's lost one leg and an arm. Bad burns. Plastic surgery on the neck and shoulders. He won't write to his family. Won't even let us write for him. His wife is coming in to-morrow. You know, Hank, if you had the time to talk to her —tell her something about your life, it would help her to understand. She is going to need a great deal of patience— and fortitude."

Rabbi Neumann's request was not the sort you could turn down.

Nor was Father Antonine's telephone call a few minutes later: "Can you make rounds with me tonight, Hank? I've got four men in Ward Thirty-six you just have to see. . . ."

A frown creased the forehead of Blanford as my telephone shrilled again. This time it was a Red Cross worker from Forest Glen. "We've got ten men on the waiting list out here for your driving class. When can you take them?"

"Class meets today. Send over two new ones and the boy who started Monday."

The letter to Elaine stayed in my pocket during my hastily gobbled lunch. Afterward I started around the wards.

In Sixty-four Al Miller was lying flat, a sheet pulled up to his neck. His head brushed the headrails, and his one leg extended clear to the foot of the bed. I thought he was asleep, but he called an obscenity as I passed. His face was flushed.

I came back and sat down. "I see you're in good humor."

"Get off my bed, that's against regulations."

"Behave yourself, soldier, or I'll hit you with your bed pan."

He grinned. "Stop giving me that chaplain talk."

"What's the big idea," I said, "trying to play sick and get out of your driving lesson?"

"Hell, no. My heel started draining again. Doc says strictly bed rest for three days."

"The government girls will miss you."

Al was a living refutation of man's mortality. He had been hit by 88 mm. shellfire in North Africa where he was with the Combat Engineers. The force of the explosion blew off one leg, loaded the mutilated stump and his good leg with assorted sizes of shrapnel, and seared his face and large areas of his body with phosphorus burns. More than once, in the months since, they had thought Al would die. Revisions (or surgery) on his stump, painful skin grafts, and the demoralization of living with a gangrenous foot had not licked him. Now they were convinced he would live. He certainly wanted to.

After a superficial visit through three wards I returned to the office and my stack of mail and telephone messages. I could ignore the scraps of paper spindled there, but I could not ignore the insistent ringing of the telephone.

Red Cross Public Relations called and wanted to know what arrangements I was making for photographers and press releases at the amputees' dance.

"Press releases? Who cares? This dance is for the men, not the newspapers. . . . All right, I'd suggest you call the Director's office. They can probably help you."

One of the recreation workers called. "What about decorations?"

"Just bring twenty or thirty Red Cross girls. They'll be decoration enough."

Then I called the recreation worker from Virginia. "Do you mind if I refer all queries on the dance to you? I'm swamped."

After she agreed and hung up, I looked across at Blanford's impassive face. "How's the war going? I haven't seen a newspaper in weeks."

Just then Jerry called from the door. He had on a new uniform and walked very well with the aid of two canes. I couldn't look at this sandy-haired young man who was just getting used to two artificial limbs without a self-conscious catch in my throat.

"I'm on my way, Hank. Just wanted to say good-by."

"You've already thrown away your crutches. Soon you'll be walking with one cane." I was echoing Dorsch's words of so many years before, as I walked with him to the drive where the cab waited. His luggage was already inside.

A small crowd had gathered to say good-by—orderlies, two nurses, a doctor, and a couple of patients.

I turned away brimming with happiness as Jerry's cab disappeared down the drive and the seers-off returned to their buildings.

Now I must get to my driving class. . . .

Lessons in handling an automobile seemed to be one of the most important factors in rehabilitating our amputees. The majority of them came from rural areas where the ability to drive a car was practically a necessity if a man was to hold a job and get along in the day-to-day life of his community. It was before the days of the automatic shift, and everyone had to learn to drive using the clutch and shifting by hand.

At the parking lot I started the old Dodge which a Washington society woman had donated to us. Then I drove to the administration building and picked up three of my pupils. When we reached the quiet corner of the grounds where we would have the lesson, the three additional ones from Forest Glen were waiting for us. The Motor Corps girl who had driven them over waved from the station wagon.

While my old students demonstrated their prowess at backing, turning, and parking on a stretch of pavement, I sat on a bench and gave "ground training" to my two new recruits.

"At first you will not be able to gauge the acceleration, since you cannot feel the pedals. You will have to learn to listen to the motor noise. . . . Afterward, when you drive in traffic, it will be difficult to hear. But you'll learn. . . ." It was all there, Dorsch's lesson, except for the German accent.

At eleven thirty that night I finished my ward calls and left the post. I breathed deeply of the fresh night air, trying to forget the chemical smell of antiseptics and the fuzzy sweet odor of gangrene. Walking through the quiet streets on the rim of Rock Creek park with its thick foliage, I thought of Elaine again and the letter which was still in my pocket. It meant so much for me to have her come to the dance that I hardly dared think about it. It meant so much for me to introduce her to the men. Elaine was to be a sort of guarantee that life awaited them back home with their families and their sweethearts.

Her letter was propped on the hall table under the lamp.
I tore it open before I climbed the stairs. . . . Good, she
would come. The weariness of the day left me as I thought
of a sure tomorrow.

Mrs. Hahn knocked at my door. "May I come in, Mr. Viscardi?"

"Of course."

"I brought you some cookies." She waved a veined finger
at me. "Young man, you're working much too hard."

It was fun having this sweet little old lady fuss over me.

"Elaine's coming to the dance!"

"How nice. I'll have everything ready for her. Can you
stay overnight at the hospital?"

"Yes. It's all arranged."

"How is everything going with those boys?"

"Something pretty nice happened today." Then I told Mrs.
Hahn about the boy whose father I had had to tell about
his losing his leg.

His name was Smitty, and he came from an isolated area
in the Tennessee hills. The other men teased Smitty about
never having seen a flush toilet before he reached a camp in
Georgia.

Reading and writing were not Smitty's long suit, so I had
been taking care of his correspondence with his family. But
he was insistent that I not reveal the secret of his amputation.
I finally hit upon the solution of telling them that Smitty
was making a good recovery from his wounds but that I felt
it would be very good for him if they could come to Washington on a visit.

I had met his father in the lounge of the Red Cross building—a rangy, weather-beaten man who looked uncomfortable
wearing a shirt with a collar. I tried to lead him gently into

the news which I was sure would be a shock, but when I told him he did not even look surprised.

"Lost a leg, has he? What's so bad about that? Rest of him's in good shape, hain't it?"

Then I took Smitty's father to the ward.

After Mrs. Hahn said good night, I sat down to finish the letter to Elaine.

I picked up the story of Jerry. Elaine had already heard the early part, about how Jerry had been injured. It was doubly hard for him. He had been a staff sergeant on duty in the United States. He had a pass to go home and a battalion truck stopped to pick him up. He slung his bag over the tailboard and was about to scramble up after it when another truck from the outfit crushed him. That afternoon at the station hospital they amputated both his legs, above the knees.

Then they sent for his parents.

There were months in the station hospital, and eventually the amputation wards at Walter Reed. Besides having lost both legs, Jerry was beset by all the problems that can badger an ordinary amputee. Gangrene, surgery on his stumps, traction, waiting, waiting, waiting for his artificial limbs. But worse than that was the thought of going home to his small town and facing the questions of his friends. "I didn't even lose my legs in a shooting war. I'm half a man and not that much of a hero," Jerry complained to me.

One day as I sat by his bed he told me about the plan the old leg maker in the prosthetic appliance shop had suggested. He wanted to make Jerry a small cart, close to the ground, so that he could propel himself with his hands. They had done that, he said, for a man in the First World War.

"That's all I need," Jerry said. "Then they can give me a cup and some pencils and I'll be set for life."

He turned his face away, but he could not stifle the sound of his sobbing.

I talked to his doctor. "You're not going to let them put Jerry on a cart, are you?"

"No, I think something can be worked out."

When the surgery was healed, they set him up on pylons. These were short wooden caps with leather cuffs which were laced over the ends of his stumps. Eventually he learned to balance himself and walk on them with the help of short canes.

"I can walk," he exulted. "But, Hank, how did you ever get used to being only *so* tall?"

"Keep at it," I said. "You won't have to get used to it. Don't forget that for one minute. You're going to have real legs."

When his limbs were ready, we worked hard. Besides the regular walking class given by the hospital, I went with him into the woods, over the lawns, on gravel paths, over curbs, up steps and down ramps. Jerry, who had been a star basketball player, drove himself like an athlete in training.

One day Jerry and I had dinner in town. We went to a good restaurant and ordered cocktails, food, wines. It was a friendly mellow evening. After dinner, as we stood shoulder to shoulder at the urinals in the men's room, Jerry suddenly said, "Gee, I could never have reached up to this thing when I was walking around on those blocks."

He had a completely sympathetic audience, for I could still remember my chagrin in the same situation years before.

We laughed as I told him.

Jerry had put off thinking about going home until a few weeks ago when he was advised that he soon would be ready for discharge.

"What am I going to do, Hank? I'm scared. I can't face

the people at home. You've seen my family's letters—there's a broken heart in every paragraph."

I agreed to go out to Pennsylvania and visit his family. When I telephoned his father, who was the superintendent of schools in the small community where they lived, he said he would be glad to see me.

The night I arrived, it was cold and rainy. Protected from the weather by my trenchcoat, I walked up the railroad platform looking for Jerry's father. The only persons there were two men who ignored me as I passed. When I returned, one of them spoke.

"Mr. Viscardi?"

"Yes."

"I didn't recognize you. I expected someone with a much more pronounced limp."

"Well," I said, "I had these things oiled today and they're running away from me."

When I got a chance to size up the husky friend whom Jerry's father introduced, I realized they had been prepared for anything. Probably they had a stretcher tucked away in the car.

Late into the night I talked with Jerry's parents. The townspeople had made big preparations for the boy's homecoming. There would be a parade up Main Street, with the high school band, marchers from civic organizations. Heaps of pity to be showered upon him. Worst of all, the council had voted him a job as tax collector, which he was practically assured of holding for life. An easy job at a salary that would meet his simple needs as he spent his days in a chair in the sun.

It was hard to tell these well-meaning people that they were wrong. When I had them convinced, there was still the rest of the community. So we hired the moving picture theater for the next night, canceled the show, and I addressed a mass meeting.

Anyway, I was able to write to Elaine tonight:

Jerry's going home today, and Jerry is going to be all right. They've agreed not to have the parade. That's the way Jerry wants it. He's going home on two legs—not as a hero for an hour, but as a citizen for the rest of his life. And Jerry isn't having any town dole of a tax collector's job. He's planning to start his own business—a hardware store.

The postscript to my letter to Elaine was written a few years later by Jerry himself when he paid off his loan from the bank and began to make plans to build a larger store as soon as his lease was up.

At the end of the letter, I said:

Darling, you don't know how happy I am that you are coming to the dance. Aside from the pleasure of your very charming company for two whole days, it will mean so much to me in a deeper sense. It will mean a lot to the boys too—to meet you and talk to you and know that girls like you are real. But I think you understand.

10

Out of Step

I sneaked into the Officers' Mess at Forest Glen at seven thirty A.M. for a cup of coffee. Fortunately this mess was more rambling than the one at Walter Reed and there was less possibility of my being noticed. There were no Red Cross dignitaries around, and no brass. I wondered if anybody would ask to see my credentials. If they did, it would be fun to watch the expression on their face when I said, "I don't have any. Absolutely none."

It had been a month since the Red Cross had removed me from the staff, after a final warning that I must make the required reports and attend meetings.

I had failed. Now that it was too late I could see it. A little more co-operation with the Red Cross, a little more diplomacy in my contacts with the Army—and I might still be in good favor.

When the Red Cross officials said, "The job that you are trying to do is not included in our manual," I had continued to go my way. A person with more tact would have written up a new job analysis and gone through channels to have it approved. I could even have given them statistics and case histories had I not been so stubborn.

But the pressure of the hundreds of men waiting to learn to walk, asking for advice with their problems, had blinded me to everything but the acute emergency.

When the Army major called me in, I had not been tactful.

"Mr. Viscardi, I know you're here to do a good job, but the attendance at our walking classes is falling off. I have been advised that you are giving lessons. What is your professional standing?"

I flared back with "I taught myself and I'll balance that as far as walking goes against any master's degree in physical therapy."

"We have certain regulations to follow . . ."

I could see now that I should have suggested, "Let me talk to your physical therapists. Perhaps I can explain some of the problems a man faces in learning to walk." Instead, I had been childish and headstrong. As a result I was told, "Henceforth, you will not give walking lessons."

The same thing had happened with the leg shop. I had gone to the colonel in charge and complained. "The men you have working here are hopelessly incompetent. They are turning out an inferior product that falls apart at the joints."

He explained to me that the Medical Corps and the Surgeon General's office only attempted to give the men temporary legs, so that they could be discharged and fitted to permanent limbs by the Veterans Administration.

"Your system of temporary legs is no good!" I stormed. "If the first limb doesn't fit, a man may never try to walk."

With more patience, I might have convinced them of the importance of rehabilitating the men as soon as possible. I knew that with a flimsy, ill-fitting leg a man's physical adjustment could be almost insurmountable and the psychological adjustment even impossible.

Theirs was a long-range program, but I was convinced that immediate attention of the best type available was required.

I did not go to General Marietta—it seemed to me it would be a waste of time.

As I finished my coffee it occurred to me that I could probably go on living on this post indefinitely—bunking in the chaplains' quarters, working underground as I had been now for a month, sneaking into the Enlisted Men's Mess once a week to fill up, keeping out of the way of a few people. Why, I could stay till the end of the war, until the weekly convoys of men with their arms and legs blown off, magically stopped rolling into the railroad yards, until everybody went home and they gave this place back to the girls.

I walked across the lawn which had once been part of the campus of National Park Seminary, a school for fashionable young women. Everything seemed out of focus. Two Red Cross Gray Ladies rounded the porch of the Japanese pagoda that had been an ornament of the original campus. A legless soldier hobbled on crutches across the bridge over the moat of the castle that had once housed young-hearted schoolgirls, and a sergeant with his arms full of duffle stood in front of the opera house that had been brought over a stone at a time from Italy. The sergeant was staring up and down as though looking for a street sign.

They seemed as out of place here as I.

I should write to Elaine today. I had put it off for a week now, but it was hard to find anything to say. The everyday things I could safely write about were not really of Elaine's world.

That dance for the amputees, for example, so many months ago, had been a success. The Red Cross girls had started dancing classes afterward, and I had typed up a manual of instructions. The men had cheered. Yes, there had been changes since the dance, particularly in my life.

It had begun like a college football week end. I had met Elaine at Union Station Saturday noon and we shared a cab to Walter Reed with a soldier, his bride, and an Army nurse. Elaine loved Mrs. Hahn's pleasant house at the edge of the golf course in Rock Creek Park. When I showed her my room, which Mrs. Hahn had transformed with fresh curtains and a bowl of zinnias, she had looked pleased.

"How's my girl?"

"Fine—oh, don't muss my hair." But she really didn't mean it.

I took Elaine for a drive through the suburbs settled among the Maryland woods and hills, and when we came back we left the old Dodge outside the Officers' Mess and went in for dinner. Then I took her up to the wards to introduce her to the men.

A nurse was just coming out of the glassed-in isolation section at one end of sixty-four, carrying a basin. Through the open door you could hear the sound of a man groaning. Elaine looked at me like a frightened bird. I squeezed her hand and glanced questioningly toward the nurse.

"He'll be all right. Just coming out of surgery," she said.

Up near the middle of the ward there was a crowd around Al Miller's bed: two girls, and three or four patients in bathrobes.

"How are you, Mike?" The boy I spoke to was drinking straight whisky from a paper cup. His smooth-shaven cheeks were blue from his heavy beard. "This is Elaine."

"*I'm* fine!" Al shouted from the bed. "This is Sally—" and he pulled one of the girls, giggling, across his chest. "Careful, honey, don't spill that drink. That's nine-week-old Scotch. Get up, now, wanta see Hank's girl. She's pretty. Much too good to hang around with an old beat-up amputee like Hank. Young woman, I warn you—"

Elaine's cry was drowned in the confusion. I think I was the only one who heard it. She had been watching the boy in the next bed pull himself up by the head bars, then swing over the side and reach his good foot to the floor. From his rolled-up pajama leg protruded a naked stump.

"We've got to make a few more stops." I put my arm around her shoulders and led her away. She was biting her lip.

A call from a bed across the ward stopped us. "This is Sims, Elaine."

"Howdy, Miss." He spoke gaily, though his mouth was pulled out of shape by a leathery burn scar that covered half his face. I followed Elaine's eyes. The spread on Sims' bed closely outlined his body, revealing unmistakably that both legs stopped just below the hips.

"Hello—uh, Sims."

"Hi, Chaplain. Doin' a little morale work on the wards?"

The speaker was a man of about forty, with one leg in a cast strung up almost perpendicularly and attached to an overhead pulley. He laid down his newspaper. One arm was about six inches long, with a healed pink scar and a row of red dots just above where the elbow should have been. It looked indecent lying there on the sheet.

"This is Jonesy."

"Nice to meet your girl, Hank. Believe me, Miss, if I was out of this squirrel cage nothing could keep me away from that dance tonight."

Elaine's reaction was that of someone who has been submerged in ice water. Her pale chilliness persisted throughout the evening, although she danced perfectly and smiled often and said all of the proper things to the General and the staff members and patients.

As we walked across the drive, she clutched my arm.

"There's—oh, there's something in those bushes. It moved!"

I laughed out loud. Then I whispered, "Just a soldier and his date."

"Do you mean those amputees—the patients—go out with girls?"

A string inside me jerked my mouth shut. I could not reply.

When we got outside the gate, Elaine turned to me, her face shadowy in the street light. "Hank, for heaven's sake, say something. Talk. Sing. Do anything!" Then she started to cry. I held her in my arms, trying to quiet her.

"Stop crying. You'll make yourself sick. Here—it's a good thing I have a spare handkerchief."

Elaine dabbed at her eyes and sniffled. "I didn't realize it would be so horrible." Her breath caught on a sob.

"What do you mean?"

"Seeing those poor men up in the ward—and then the ones who were trying to dance. How can they stand to live like that?"

"You're talking to one of them."

"Well, you—you're different." But she spoke without conviction.

Elaine had stopped crying by the time we reached Mrs. Hahn's, but the lingering good night I had planned was forgotten. Early the next morning she took a train to New York.

I still showed her picture to the men—the pretty snapshot in my wallet that was as worn and frayed as an outdated credit card. And though we had had pleasant evenings together the two times I had been home on leave since the dance, the enchantment was broken.

The last time, Mamma had asked, "Is something wrong between you and Elaine?"

"No, of course not." I was sure that when I got out of the service and was seeing her every day things would be better.

Mamma eyed me sharply. "Henry, you look tired."

Today I would write to Elaine. I would tell her about the spring flowers in the park, and the magnolia trees that were blooming around Forest Glen. I would tell her—oh, what would I tell her?

There was a batch of letters for me on Father Antonine's desk with a scribbled note: "Meet me for lunch at 12—A." That clerk in the hospital post office must still be sneaking my mail out to the chaplains' box.

DEAR HANK:

Well, I'm home. They had me speak at the Rotary Club yesterday. I'm quite a curiosity here, you'd think I had three heads. Except that if I had three heads I could get a job in the circus. Nobody here has come up with an offer yet. . . . My mother says to wait a while. She doesn't understand . . .

HI VISCARDI, OLD PADRE!

I'm getting to be quite a pinochle player. That's all I do beside cash my pension checks. What in hell am I going to do with my life? Nobody seems to realize I want to earn a living and get married and raise a family . . .

DEAR MR. VISCARDI:

My son Ronald tells me you are the one at Walter Reed who seems to understand his problems and that you have some good ideas to help amputees if you only had a chance to work them out.

I'm writing to my congressman . . .

The letters were the same every day. I answered them on Father Antonine's portable typewriter and filed them in the cardboard case I kept in a corner of the room.

Then I went out to the pay telephone in the corridor and called Colonel Howard Rusk's office at the Pentagon.

"Your appointment is for four thirty," a sergeant said.

As I walked outside the hospital grounds to mail my letters, it occurred to me that Dr. Rusk might not be entirely prepared for my visit. Maybe he would be surprised that I had fumbled my job. I hoped he wouldn't think I was letting him down. He was a pretty fair guy though: I had realized that the first time I met him, several weeks ago.

"It was nice of you to come, Mr. Viscardi," he had said.

"Quite the contrary, Dr. Rusk. It's a pleasure to meet a man who understands rehabilitation." I had heard of the Air Force's Convalescent Training Division, which he headed. He had started with a rehabilitation setup for pneumonia patients that was getting them back on active duty sooner than ever before. Then he had gone down the line and revised rehabilitation procedures for the wounded.

Even the loyal enthusiasm of the Air Force boys I had met at Walter Reed had not prepared me for this man, who, in addition to his commanding physical presence, seemed to possess powerful reserves of mind and spirit.

"I've heard reports about you, Dr. Rusk, from your pilots who are patients over at the amputation center."

Rusk chuckled boyishly. "They've brought me reports on you too. They tell me you are teaching the men to walk. Now I'd like to hear your report on Walter Reed. A lot of our men get funneled into the amputation center and we can't get our hands on them."

"I can give you a report, Doctor, but not a favorable one."

"Let's hear it."

I told him that I felt Walter Reed had been poorly prepared to meet the problem of the great volume of amputees. With their good medical men, advanced surgical procedures, and modern equipment, they had stopped short when it came to rehabilitation.

Their tiny prosthetics shop was a joke. I talked about the

limb maker who wanted to build a cart for Jerry; about the men who had to wait weeks for limbs, and the legs they got which were only temporary and of inferior quality.

"Why don't they take a tip from the Germans?" I said. "I saw a beautiful limb on an exchanged POW a few weeks ago. It was wood, but it was well made and it fitted. Why, even the concentration-camp job one of them had, made of tin cans soldered together, fitted better than the things we give them."

On top of that, I told Dr. Rusk, the amputation center had no well-integrated program for the men. They needed many more physical therapists, and the ones already on the staff did not understand the problems involved in learning to walk with an artificial limb. The men got discouraged and nobody did much about it. Then they went home on furlough and the communities finished the job. They got pity, pensions, doles, but no respect.

"It's disgraceful," I concluded. "Why should we spend millions to fight this war if we aren't going to give our wounded men a chance to become productive citizens again!"

I dropped my letters in a street mailbox and went back to the chaplains' quarters.

Father Antonine was waiting for me. "How would you like to drive over to Silver Spring for lunch?"

"I know—you have a yen for one of those strawberry sundaes."

"Could be," he said. "Are you going to the Pentagon today? You may have my car if you'll drop me at Walter Reed."

"That will be very nice. I have to stop there too."

The pleasure of watching Father Antonine down a dish of ice cream in his husky, youthful fashion was spoiled today by my thoughts.

"What's on your mind, Hank? Or don't you want to tell me?"

"I'm licked, Father Antonine."

"You know you are welcome to stay as long as I am here."

"That would be all right if I had the spirit for the job, but it's so endless."

"Nevertheless, you are doing good work."

"It's not enough, Father Antonine. Even if I could get the Red Cross to see things my way—let me come out of the cellar and handle my own program instead of following a lot of rules that were set up for the Civil War—I couldn't accomplish what has to be done."

He waited.

"I'm convinced that the rehabilitation of these amputees has got to be followed through in the communities. You've seen the letters they write back. They can't lead normal lives even when they leave this place." I pounded my fist on the rickety table and the dishes rattled.

"Do you think it's any kindness to teach a man to walk, to give him back his self-confidence, and then to have industry slap him in the face when he tries to earn a living? I've worked hard—and for what!"

"Easy, my boy. These things must come slowly." Father Antonine was not giving me any clerical double talk. He was speaking as a person who has seen two wars, the first one as a fighting man. "Remember, whatever you sacrifice goes to help make another life stronger."

"If I only had your faith—" I said. "It gives you strength. I remember I felt it that night you took me to the Franciscan House of Studies."

Father Antonine and all the other Franciscan chaplains in the Washington area had been invited to the monastery for evening services and supper. As Father Antonine's guest I was the only layman there, and I had a lot of difficulty convincing a rather aged friar that I was not Father Viscardi. He had mistaken the Red Cross emblems on my lapels for a chaplain's insignia. The simple food passed down the long table in bowls, the silent men at the board, and the reading aloud of prayers during the meal took me a thousand miles and years away from Washington and the war. In this quiet little world that had no geographic identity I was back at Fordham again. There was time to rest and time to think. Yes, and time to work.

Father Antonine's spoon clattered in the empty ice cream dish. "Time to go, Hank, if we are to keep our appointments."

In the parking lot he gave me the keys to his car and I agreed to pick him up after dinner.

I met four men back of the administration building and drove them to a remote corner of the hospital grounds. There, in the woods, I held my unofficial walking class. What a thrill it was to watch these clumsy-looking youths gradually catch the rhythm of the step, and finally put away their crutches and canes.

"You don't need to come any more," I said to Major Robinson. "You graduate today."

After class, when we were returning to the building, Robbie walked with me.

"How did you like Mrs. Roosevelt?" he said.

"She was wonderful. Boy, you certainly gave me a build-up with her."

Robbie, who was a fighter pilot, had been entertained at the White House a short time before with his friend Ted Lawson, who wrote *Thirty Seconds Over Tokyo*. He laughed. "I only said, 'Hank Viscardi taught me how to walk—I'm afraid he may be forced to leave us.'"

The invitation to the White House was a complete surprise. I received a message to call a certain number. When I got the extension Malvina Thompson answered. She said, "Mrs. Roosevelt would like to invite you to tea day after tomorrow at three thirty."

It was ironical, I thought, that this command invitation from the First Lady should come at a time when I was cadging meals at various messes—yes, even at a monastery.

But when I had been admitted to Mrs. Roosevelt's sitting room—after having my name checked off a list by the man at the gate house on Pennsylvania Avenue, the guard who opened the front door, and the elevator man—all thought of food left me. For I faced one of the the most charming women I have ever met.

"I hear you're doing some wonderful work," she said graciously.

"I'm not so sure, Mrs. Roosevelt."

"I have heard reports. Tell me, are you having difficulty in putting your program over?"

This great lady so inspired my confidence that before I realized it I was telling her my story. Not the whole story—I omitted the part about Elaine.

She listened thoughtfully.

An hour later a secretary interrupted. "Mrs. Roosevelt, your appointment with ——."

"In a moment," she said. "Will you please ask him to wait?"

I finished by telling Mrs. Roosevelt, "The system just isn't geared for this emergency. We must change it."

She smiled. "These are trying times, but I'm sure the problems will be worked out."

I believed her. "Of course," I said, "if this system can be changed, there's an even greater need outside. I'd like to talk to people in industry."

"When you are ready," she said, "let me know. I think perhaps I can help you." . . .

Robbie and I had reached Ward G-6, where he lived, by the time I finished telling him about my conversation with Mrs. Roosevelt. "Keep your fingers crossed," I said as I left him. "I think there will be some changes."

From there I went up to the disciplinary ward. Before entering I made sure there was no brass around.

Al Miller was sitting up in bed, fully clothed except for his leg, reading a twenty-five-cent novel with a half-nude girl on the cover.

"Another hour and you wouldn't have found me here."

"Your sentence up?"

"Four weeks, for Christ's sake."

"Do you realize that sweeping you up was my last official act?"

"Don't carry on like that. You're breakin' my heart."

Al had gotten me out of bed at Mrs. Hahn's in the middle of the night. "Hank, I'm in trouble. Leg broke down. Whad'll I do?"

"Where are you?" I said sleepily into the phone.

"Willard Hotel—I think."

"Well, pick up all the pieces and call a taxicab and stop at my place."

My carefully made plans failed. I got Al past the MP and up to the ward and into bed. An hour later, however, he raised such a fuss and gave such a robust dissertation on the Army and its artificial limbs that he was shipped down to the disciplinary ward.

Al nodded toward the next bed. "Getta load of that guy. He's griping because they took his leg away to keep him in this joint. For Christ's sake, I tell him it's better than having the damn thing busted up for kindling like mine. It wouldn't matter so much only Babe's coming down next week end. You know how women are."

Babe was the only girl Al didn't joke about.

I recognized the man in the next bed as one of the POW's who had come in on the last convoy. They were a disciplinary problem in any man's army. Heroes, all of them—and they knew it. Like our boys going back to the little towns and farms, I thought. A hero has to be different.

After I left Al, as I was passing through one of the sun porches with its afternoon crowd of crap shooters and men in wheel chairs listening to the ball game on portable radios, somebody grabbed my arm.

A boy with a sunburned face looked at me through bloodshot eyes.

"Tex," I said, "thought you were home on furlough."

"Got back today."

"What are you doing in a wheel chair? Where's your limb?"

"Under the bed. Why bother? Boy, did I have a swell leave. All the liquor I could hold. Women—they were mad for me. The VFW had a dinner. Gave me a hundred-dollar bond. Soft life, Hank."

"There's more to life than that, Tex. What are you doing to yourself?"

But he just shrugged.

An hour later I was telling Dr. Rusk about it in his office at the Pentagon.

"Can't you see, Dr. Rusk? Working with these men is futile unless we can get co-operation from the community."

He nodded as I went on.

"A man's heart can be captured. Sometimes in a few minutes. Sometimes it takes weeks. He can be made to feel that he is a person again. Then a thirty-day furlough can undo it all. His disability becomes a badge of honor. They make him wear it—right around his neck."

"You're right," he said. "Do you have any ideas about reaching the community?"

"Yes, through industry. Mrs. Roosevelt has offered to help." I told him about my visit to the White House.

"What about your work at Walter Reed?"

"I'm not on the staff any more."

Rusk's face grew serious.

"The Red Cross transferred me to Massachusetts a month ago. A mere formality, I assure you. They know I won't accept."

"That's too bad," Rusk said. "Did they give you any warning?"

I laughed, but rather hollowly I'm afraid. "It was more of an ultimatum. I had trouble with the Army too—they disapproved of my walking classes. I'm not a professional therapist."

Rusk grinned. "Your therapy may not be scientific but it did a peck of good to our pilots." He looked at me. "You've been working pretty hard. When do you plan to leave Washington?"

"I'd go today if I were packed."

"Tell you what," he said, "you need a rest. I'll send you up to our rehabilitation center at Pawling for a few weeks. Fresh air, good food—you'll like it. . . . Don't thank me. Call it a bonus from the Air Forces for services rendered."

I could not answer Rusk. I was afraid my voice would give me away.

I slept fifteen hours the first day at Pawling, and got to be a real chow hound as I lined up with the intermingled officers and men for the ladlings of scrambled eggs and wedges of ham that were hurled at us by the kitchen helpers.

Three weeks later I was back in Rusk's office. He had telephoned me the night before to ask me to go with him to Hap Arnold, chief of the Air Forces, and tell my story.

"Just tell him what you told me," Rusk was saying. "We'll get some action."

Once in General Arnold's office I had the floor. Halfway through my story his round smile settled into a straight line and he began pressing buttons. Rusk and I were surrounded by a coterie of generals and staff members. There were a few colonels too.

I felt like the catalyst in an interdepartmental fizz-up, and I was enjoying it.

"Bob," Hap Arnold was addressing Robert Lovett, Assistant Secretary of War for Air, "Mr. Viscardi has important information for your office."

He nodded to General David N. Grant, Surgeon General of the Air Forces. "I'd suggest, General, that you arrange a conference with Mr. Viscardi immediately."

The snowball was gaining momentum. Even Congress got into the act. The Air Forces continued to put pressure on to improve conditions for their pilots. Meanwhile parents from all over the country were writing to their congressmen and complaining about the inadequacy of the amputee program. Walter Reed made plans to extend the shop for prosthetic appliances to three times its former size, and they hired a larger staff of physical therapists. A new amputation center was put in operation at Battle Creek, Michigan, and others were scheduled to open. Eventually, at the request of the Surgeon General's Office, the National Research Council set up a committee to work on the improvement of artificial limbs.

This was the beginning of a wonderful program set up by the armed forces and the Veterans Administration which today provides the disabled soldier with the finest prosthetic appliances the world has ever known.

I stayed around Washington for a few days to answer questions, then lit out for New York.

Dr. Rusk's parting words were, "Come over to the Air Forces and I'll give you a job."

Elaine and I sat in the glider which was moving aimlessly back and forth. It was warm for May, but she had on a thin sweater over her dress.

"So—you're a civilian again."

"No more uniforms for me," I agreed heartily. "Same old suit. . . . It's nice to be together again, isn't it?"

Elaine put her small foot to the terrace to stop our swinging. "I—of course."

There was a sickening tightness in my throat, then it plunged downward. I realized that I had somehow been counting on Elaine's accepting me again on the old basis. But I should have known. The staginess of the dinner. Her mother's undue solicitude. The buck-up-old-fellow quality of her father's handshake as he had lighted his evening cigar and strolled down to the corner for a paper. Her mother's shooing us out onto the porch in a self-conscious flutter.

"Elaine." I touched her chin lightly and turned her face toward me. "Look at me, Elaine. Will you marry me? Would you marry me tomorrow if we could?"

For a second the frightened look I had seen in her eyes that night in the ward returned. "I—well—" She began to cry silently. "I wanted to marry you—but I can't. I couldn't marry a man who has no legs. Don't make me talk about it—I just can't." She slipped off the glider and ran into the house.

For some time I sat there swinging. I could not feel the floor under my feet, and I had the sensation that the glider was moving entirely of its own accord.

Elaine's mother came to the door. Her face was in shadow behind the screen. "Don't get up," she said.

"Elaine has told you, hasn't she? It's been so terribly hard for all of us, Henry, because we like you very much."

11

"Leg Man"

"The world is full of women." Tom Slater crunched a pickle and looked carefully over his plate of cold cuts at Dunhall's, preparatory to making a selection.

Tom sounded like all the others, but for me there was only one woman, and she had turned me down. I looked dully into the bowl of cold Vîchyssoise before me.

"What is a little thing like a love affair to a man who leads the exciting life you do?" Tom said. "One day you're in Washington telling the bigwigs how to win the war and the next day I get a letter from you on Hyde Park stationery."

The visit to Hyde Park had been a pleasant interlude in a summer of discontent—the quiet garden, the talks with Mrs. Roosevelt and her other guests. Robbie must have told her about Elaine—he was there. Mrs. Roosevelt mentioned it one day. "The girl you were engaged to, Hank—it surely is a disappointment. But when you marry I think it is very important that both people have maturity and understanding of each other's problems. And when you do find the right girl you will realize what I mean."

Dr. Yanover's comments had been harsher.

"You're lucky," he said. "The marriage would never have worked. She was completely unrealistic—she pitied you. You can't base a marriage on pity."

Doc's words were not very comforting. I had been thrown over by my girl. My work with the Army was a big question mark. My efforts on behalf of the disabled had become feeble and dispirited. I dragged myself through the tiring days, and the pain had returned to my limbs.

"I'm going to give you some advice, Hank, though I don't know whether you will have sense enough to take it. Stop racing your motor. Stop being a crusader. You've lost weight. You're run down. You're killing yourself."

I heard what he said, but it did not seem to matter.

All at once the lines of his face relaxed and he brightened with the light of discovery. "I know what's wrong with you. You're wallowing in self-pity. You think you've been unfortunate in a love affair simply because you're crippled. Did it ever occur to you that men with two legs get this sort of treatment every day? It's happened to me—more than once." He grinned. "Some day you'll meet a wonderful girl. I guarantee it. Now do me a favor. Go and get yourself a job. Something you'd like to do. Turn your back on your cause for a while. You can always return to it."

"What brings you into New York on this fine August day?" Tom Slater said, as he set down his coffee cup. "A conference with the Mayor?"

I laughed. "No, I'm through with conferences for the time being."

There had been plenty of conferences after I was released from the Red Cross. At Tom's urging, I told him about my trial run in industry.

Mrs. Roosevelt had kept her promise and in May had arranged for me to return to Washington and see James

Carey, national secretary-treasurer of the CIO. I was impressed that Carey was such a young man. He seemed to have a keen appraisal of the situation.

"These disabled veterans are returning to their homes," I said. "Many of them are able to work, but they aren't getting jobs. I'd like to know whether organized labor will co-operate in putting them back to work."

"You certainly have my personal support, and I can get you the blessing of Phil Murray," he said. "As far as the CIO is concerned, the problem has to be worked out in each plant with the help of the local union. We can make suggestions, though."

He wished me luck and I went over to the WPB where Mrs. Roosevelt had made an appointment for me with Charles Wilson, its director, who was on loan from his job as president of General Electric. His hospitality echoed the comfortable environment of his big office. An American flag stood near his desk and a map of the United States covered one wall. He offered me a large cigar, which I declined. I was afraid to smoke it. I had been a chain cigarette smoker in the Walter Reed days, but since then had reverted to the pipe I had adopted when I started sailing.

"Do you have any specific plan?" he asked.

"I don't know. I'd like to go into the fields of commerce and industry and see what I can do to change the thinking."

He agreed with me that by putting disabled veterans to work in jobs that fitted their capacities, industry would increase the purchasing power of the community and lower the relief budget. "It's enlightened selfishness to hire these men," he said.

Wilson sent me to General Electric for talks with management, and paved the way for me to approach General Motors and other industries. I had some friendly interviews. Everybody agreed that the plan was foolproof, on the surface. I even got to see the aircraft people; Dr. Rusk and the Aircraft War Production Council arranged that.

Also, I went to work in some plants. There, some of the reasons underlying the problem became apparent. The people at the top had time to talk to me, but once in the din of the assembly line, I discovered that everybody from the plant superintendent on down was so busy pounding out the products required by the greedy war machine, that other problems seemed unimportant.

Through the personnel department of a Long Island aircraft factory I arranged to be hired in a series of jobs, so that I could conduct my investigations unofficially. The first day I walked into the hangar-sized room where fighter planes were being assembled, it sounded to me as though all of the two or three hundred workers were filing on aluminum with pieces of iron. It occurred to me that in a job here deafness might be no drawback. In fact, if you were not deaf when you started, it was a sure thing you would be by the end of a week.

"How do those two cats sleep?" I asked the foreman, by gestures and exaggerated lip movement.

He spoke close to my ear. "They get used to it. Lot of mice around—that's why we have them."

My first job was in the tool crib where I had charge of distributing small parts, tools, bits, and jigs. Sometimes the men or women called at the window with chits; I made regular rounds to deliver others.

Later, when I was working in the foundry making molds, I found that having to work close to the floor made the job very difficult because of my unkneeling limbs. But there were many jobs that I could do as well as the other workers—cleaning up castings, polishing, and handling a spray gun in the paint shop.

One day my foreman said, "I notice you limping. Anything wrong?"

"Nothing serious."

At the end of three weeks the personnel director and the plant superintendent called a meeting. The director of training and nine or ten supervisors and foremen were there, along with some of the top men in charge of production.

"Hank," the plant superintendent nodded toward me, "has been making a special study to determine whether any of the jobs here can be handled by disabled veterans." He turned to one of the supervisors. "What would your reaction be to having an amputee in your department?"

The man shook his head. "Wouldn't work."

"If you men don't mind, I'd like to have you repeat what you told me the other day." Then he asked each of my foremen in turn whether my work had been satisfactory. They all replied in the affirmative.

"It may surprise you," the superintendent said, "to know that Hank is an amputee. In fact, he has two artificial limbs."

"I'll be damned," one of them said. "I never would have known it."

Then I gave my report, suggesting minor changes that would make it possible for many of the jobs to be handled by persons with physical impairments. "You might use some stools at those drill presses," I said to one supervisor. And to another—"If that bench in the foundry were higher, less bending would be required."

Everybody agreed that perhaps something could be done. We shook hands all around.

Something was done. In a few isolated spots disabled veterans were being employed efficiently, but more often the projects failed. I discovered a lack of planning on the part of most of the industries. With heavy wartime production schedules to meet, expediency was the rule. Thus, they were not fully measuring the abilities of the incapacitated. They would give a blind man a job sorting various-sized bolts into compartments, when the blind man had a master's degree in economics and mathematics. Although he could perform this small job with extreme dexterity, he was not being used to the fullest extent of his abilities.

Industry did not seem to understand the distinction between physical and occupational disability. Actually less than one per cent of the population is physically fit for all kinds of work. Most of us have a physical impairment of some sort. Frequently this disability is not a bar to the person's doing a particular job. A girl with an artificial limb may be an excellent secretary. She is *physically* disabled but not *occuppationally disabled* with respect to her particular job. A man who is a perfect physical specimen, on the other hand, and is a graduate engineer, may be *occupationally* disabled for a job as secretary because he lacks the training and special abilities to perform it.

One of the greatest shocks, though, was the occasional case of a plant making a certain department a dumping ground. A manager would point proudly to the fact that "everybody in our supply room is incapacitated," or "we use only blind men in this operation." They were literally setting up "countries of the blind," ghettos for the physically disabled.

Why must industry divide the world into the blessed and the damned? Couldn't they look on them as people with varying degrees of industrial fitness? Suddenly I was sick of seeing and talking and thinking about the physically disabled. I was sick of myself. Who did I think I was, trying to reform the world with my feeble program?

"The results of my work with industry haven't been sensational," I told Tom. "I think I'm going to look for a job."

"How about HOLC?"

"I can go back there, but I'd rather try something new."

We had finished our lunch when he said casually, "Hank, have you ever thought of working in radio?"

"I don't know a thing about it."

"That makes you an expert. I'm going to have to hire another assistant. If you're interested, come upstairs and talk to my boss."

I became Assistant to the Director of Special Events and Sports at Mutual Broadcasting Corporation. The title was not used officially. I was just a "leg man" for Tom Slater.

"What am I supposed to do?" I asked him when I reported on the first of September.

"Just follow me around for a few days. I'll show you."

"Special Events and Sports" included all sorts of things—a big bond rally with the personal appearance of a movie star, a prize fight at Madison Square Garden, a concert from Carnegie Hall with Leopold Stokowski on the podium, a World Series ball game. Wherever Tom had a broadcast scheduled I went along to help with preparations. I might spend two days in Philadelphia getting Navy clearances and checking on the technical arrangements for his description of the launching of a new aircraft carrier. In advance of a big semi-official dinner, I might have to telephone the offices of the Secretary of the Treasury, the Governor, and the Russian Ambassador for copies of their speeches; then the day of the banquet I would go over to the Waldorf Astoria to be sure our lines were installed and the program was on and off as planned.

Perhaps I'd be hanging around the office after work, chatting with the night man, as I was one evening when we got news of a hurricane that was drenching the New England coast and chewing up docks and scattering fishing boats and cruisers as it went. We called the flood area on the teletype and asked our local station what the chances were for a pick-up that night. They advised us: "Have field unit in operation with emergency squad. Believe we can give you ten minutes at nine o'clock."

Then we telephoned Chicago, which was scheduled to pipe dance music throughout the network from nine to ten. They agreed to release the network stations in the eastern section of the country on cue, for the hurricane broadcast. "We'll send the dance music to the western half," they decided, since the storm was chiefly of sectional news interest.

I was fascinated to discover how much preparation goes into a show, and how many people may be involved in filling in ten or fifteen minutes of radio time. The hard part of my job was cuing in segments of programs from various parts of the country and having the whole thing run smoothly. The stop watch became my very life. And once I made a terrible mistake: I fed a glamour shampoo commercial to the farmers who were waiting to hear about agricultural salt for their livestock.

One of the biggest returns for me was that through my work on broadcasts of athletic events I became eligible to join the Sports Broadcasters Association. I can see now that the thrill of attending weekly luncheons with men like Ted Husing and Bill Stern, where stars of baseball and football were honored guests, was a reliving of the high school days when I associated with the big athletes of the varsity teams.

In this exciting new life there was still one important link with the prewar self—the *Eph Tutt*.

She was the *Eph Tutt VI*, a pretty little sloop that I had discovered, a few weeks after I came home from Washington, under a walnut tree near a deserted house at Plandome. I bought her, and with a little carpentry and some paint she was trim and seaworthy. What she needed most was a good soaking for her thirsty timbers. Again I was sailing the Sound.

One Sunday morning after six o'clock Mass, I was headed for the *Eph Tutt's* mooring and a day's sailing, when I ran into Lennie Sampson, the ship's carpenter, on the main street of Port Washington.

"Morning, Lennie. Isn't it early for you to be out?"

"Right you are, lad," he said with soft Scotch inflections, "and I'm hung over something terrible. Oh, for a drink—oh, my poor head."

"I don't think you'll have any luck finding hard liquor at this hour, but there's always coffee."

In the waterfront diner two fishermen were having ham and eggs. I ordered some breakfast and Lennie drank three large cups of black coffee.

"Ah, what a night." Lennie screwed up his leathery face, then moved his head slowly back and forth as though testing the condition of his joints. "And what a day I'm in for."

"What's the trouble?"

"I'm to meet a train and I don't know which train."

"Got company coming?"

"No, I'm selling a houseboat. You know that boat that used to swing from a mooring off the town dock? Not far from your sloop. Sid Larcom owns it, but I have a sort of interest in it. That's a secret, though."

The binges the two cronies had aboard the houseboat *Floradora* on Saturday nights, when Lennie collected his week's pay and Sid came home from fishing, were no secret as far as I was concerned. The parties usually wound up around noon on Sunday with the two of them rowing a zig-zag course to the home dock, and singing sea chanteys.

"Sid's wife thinks the houseboat is a bad influence—" Lennie's eyes were open now, and he was leaning on one elbow, speaking confidentially—"so we have to sell it."

"Who's the buyer?"

He shook his head. "That's just it. I can't remember. He

came by the shipyard last night and made me an offer. We had us a drink or two and he said he would be out on the train today. I don't know what train, and I don't remember his name. And he was a real good spender, that he was—he's ready to pay five hundred dollars."

"Perhaps I could help you out," I said. "How about showing me the houseboat? Maybe I'd like to buy it."

The houseboat was hauled up behind Oscar's Tavern in a small shipyard. The outside was in good shape, even to the railing which would keep an unsteady skipper from going over the side. A mess of bottles and beer cans littered the cabin, and I discovered that the bilge was loaded with them when Lennie lifted the trap door.

"We figured they would keep her afloat if she ever foundered," he explained.

I bought the *Floradora* and went to work on her. Under seventeen layers of paint I found the name *Shoal Waters* carved into the forward bulkhead. So I rechristened her, or rather restored her original name to her. At the end of six weeks I had put in four bunks and a galley and was living on board and commuting to the office. "The change will be good for you," Mamma said. "Come and see us when you need clean clothes and some home cooking." Lucille Bonnar and some of the other neighbors with whom I had sailed helped out with monk's cloth curtains and cushions for the cabin.

Throughout the warm weather the houseboat made a very satisfactory bachelor's quarters. Mamma and the girls came out to visit me on warm evenings—I used to drive in and pick them up in a secondhand Studebaker I had bought—but none of them would set foot on the *Eph Tutt,* which was moored alongside.

My closest neighbor was Captain Black, or Dad Black as I grew to call him. He was a sort of Santa Claus in dungarees, except for the whiskers, who lived in a big motor launch anchored nearby.

When I say "big" I am using the term conservatively. The *Ioneta* was seventy-five feet long. He had bought her following his retirement from the Merchant Marine. She was ponderous and unsightly, and her interior was cluttered with old lumber and relics of better days. Captain Black slept on deck under a tarpaulin, and she never sailed except for the times when I went along to help him pilot her.

Every morning the Captain would row me ashore in time to catch the train to New York. He would spend the day working around the boat or visiting with his seafaring friends in town, then pick me up at night.

After supper he would come over for a cup of coffee. When it was raw, we would stoke up the big stove in the cabin of the houseboat, which the Captain swore would drive a Nor'easter right off the coast. He would put his feet up on the stove and tell me about the time he was wounded delivering cargo during the invasion of North Africa; about his brother who had a farm on the seacoast of Maine, his son who was killed in the Air Force, or his daughter who was now married. When it was clear, we would take the sloop out for a sail and pass the time of day with other neighbors, or just sit under the awning on the afterdeck and watch the sunset.

Not far away was moored another sloop, belonging to a young writer. It was slightly larger than the *Eph Tutt* and had a cabin. However, it was crowded below decks and the head, which was under the deck just forward of the mast, did not permit much clearance. As a result, anyone using the toilet found that the most convenient position was with his head and shoulders protruding upward through the hatch. The arrangement provided about as much privacy as a *pissotière* on a Paris street corner.

Every week end the artist had a different woman "house guest." One rainy Sunday, Captain Black and I looked across from the shelter of our awning on the deck of *Shoal Waters* and noticed our neighbor's feminine visitor sitting with her head emerging from the hatch and an umbrella hoisted above her. She was looking around the harbor unconcernedly and seemed "happy as a clam at high tide," as the Captain put it.

I prided myself on being an early riser those mornings on the water and getting my housekeeping done before leaving for work.

One morning I decided to give the decks a coat of paint. Like a good painter, I refrained from the comic-strip error of painting myself into a corner; I carefully planned to finish up at the side where the dinghy line was made fast. But like a bad sailor, I had miscalculated the weather. Just as I was about to paint the last three square feet of deck, a spatter of rain came down. I looked desperately back to the cabin where the casement windows swung wide, and finally chose to leave them open rather than mess up my beautiful work. It was too bad my oilskins were painted into the cabin. Well, I'd call the Captain and make a quick dash for shore. In my attempt to rise from my sitting position on the deck, I swung my weight too far forward and struck a window frame with the side of my face, just below my left eye. While I was recovering my balance, my tie brushed the freshly painted wood. Then I painted my way to the ladder and climbed down to the dinghy to find it half full of water. Apparently it had rained during the night.

It poured as I rowed ashore and dripped into the closest telephone booth. I called the office and explained that I had a black eye, was covered with paint, all wet, and would not be in.

Friends from the office sometimes visited me. One time in particular was a Sunday in October. The crowd of men and girls who had come to Port Washington for a sail and dinner on the houseboat were unusually happy and carefree. The war was over. It was 1945.

I had seen her at Mutual, although I did not know her very well. She worked as a cartographer in the promotion department where she made coverage maps. Her name was Lucile Darracq. She and another girl were in the galley washing the dinner dishes.

"We're out of water, skipper." Lucile looked at me pertly.

"There was quite a bit in the tanks. Did you have it running long?" I said.

"Of course." The dimple at the side of her mouth deepened. "How else do you wash dishes?"

I got a kick out of her bright casualness.

"You city girls," I said. "Too much apartment-house living. Out here we store water in tanks. It's valuable. I won't be able to get any more till the water boat comes by tomorrow. No Sunday deliveries."

Lucile seemed interested. "Do you have it delivered like milk?"

"Yes, except that we get fifty gallons at a time. The water boat fills up our tanks."

"How sensible," she said with half a twinkle.

"Of course," I went on, swept away with my role as an old salt, "it's the same way with garbage. We don't throw it overboard. The garbage boat comes by and collects it every day."

"Intriguing," Lucile said.

This girl was not only unimpressed with my rather bombastic pronouncements, she was pretty.

Almost at once I wanted to spend more time with her. She was wholesome and pleasant, not at all affected like many of the girls on the performing side of radio or in the advertising agencies.

I invited her to a Columbia football game which I was handling for the network the following Saturday. And I took her out sailing on Sunday—but without the crowd from the studio.

"Aye, aye, skipper." Lucile made fast the jib sheet as we came about on a new tack. I was conscious of the fact that I still puffed casually on my pipe, as I swung the tiller and brought the *Eph Tutt* around, heading my profile into the wind.

But Lucile was looking out across the Sound.

"How'm I doing?" She smiled back.

"You're doing fine for a saucy female," I said, putting my arm around her. The *Eph Tutt* heeled into the wind as I hugged her impulsively. "And I love you."

As simply as that, I made the most important declaration of my life. Lucile was lovely, and I knew that I loved her.

The old apprehensions returned. I couldn't hurt her. Did I have the right to ask that she might love me? Doc had said that when the right girl came along it would not matter to her. Love and understanding would penetrate through any barrier to the real persons. Mrs. Roosevelt had said it far more eloquently that day at Hyde Park when we talked about Elaine.

Of course, they were right, but how could I be certain? If only I knew she loved me too.

The night I asked Lucile to marry me—we had heard *La Traviata* and were still surrounded by the enchantment of its lilting romantic music when we reached her house—she answered, "I don't know, Hank."

The music stopped. "Is—is it because of my legs?"

We had never discussed my problem particularly. Lucile

had known about my limbs from the first, as did the others in the office where we worked.

Her surprised look brought back my reassurance with a rush.

"Of course not. It doesn't make a bit of difference. But I think we should be sure that it will be the best thing for both of us."

A week later she said she would marry me.

There was another side to Lucile—she was romantic. I found it out when she knitted the Argyle socks for her cousin Maurice.

"Feel this wool, Hank, do you think it's soft enough? What about the colors?"

"Maurice will love them," I teased. "He is a very lucky guy."

By the time the socks were finally done, it was spring, and Lucile presented them, not to Maurice but to me, in a birthday package.

"You mean the socks weren't for Maurice after all?" I said.

Lucile shook her head slowly, a delighted twinkle in her eyes. "I fooled you."

"Honey, you're wonderful. But don't you think it's too bad to waste all this warm, soft wool on a pair of willow feet?"

Lucile's sudden startled look was my reward.

12

Stardust and Cement

Other engaged couples were facing the same problem. There just were no empty houses in 1946. The magazines were filled with cartoons about the apartment shortage. Hotel lobbies were cluttered with the luggage of incoming guests, who sat on the edge of overstuffed chairs waiting for rooms to be vacated and assigned to them. You couldn't even build a house; there was no lumber, no hardware—scarcely any nails.

One Sunday in the living room of Lucile's aunt's home in New Jersey, the two of us relaxed in after-dinner contentment lazing through newspapers and magazines. Lucile had just said "Something will turn up" for about the five-hundredth time that spring. I had agreed with her as though we were playing a child's game and resumed browsing through the *Times* radio section.

"Look, Hank!" Lucile spread a decorating magazine across my lap. I read: "We Transformed a Garage into a House— It's Easy." It was another of those articles about a young couple with more ingenuity than cash who perform impossible feats.

"Maybe we could find a garage," Lucile was saying. "I bet

we could do it. Would it be any harder for you than building boats?"

"I don't know. But where do we get the garage?"

Where indeed.

A vague idea was trying to impress itself upon my consciousness, but I did not mention it, not until the next night when I telephoned Lucile.

"I found a garage."

"No! Where?"

"Doc Yanover's."

During the war Doc and his wife, a perky little woman whom he called "Sunny," had bought an old estate adjacent to the Merchant Marine Academy at King's Point out on Long Island. They had since remodeled the big house that sat on a bluff overlooking the Sound, and made a lovely home for themselves and their two daughters. They even had their own boat-mooring and were making plans to build a swimming pool on the property as soon as materials were available.

Their garden ran uphill on the rear of the land, and at the top left-hand corner stood an old carriage house, which had been converted into a three-car garage.

"That thing?" Doc said, when I asked him. "We don't want it. I was going to have it torn down this summer. . . . Sure, bring Lucile out to look at it. *She* can live next door to me any time she wants to."

"This place is full of junk, Bob. . . . Be careful of your skirt, Lucile," Sunny Yanover said, as Doc undid the rusty lock and slid back the screeching door the following evening to admit our inspection party. We stood in the few feet that were clear by the door.

The pile of debris shut out practically all illumination from the windows. I switched on the flashlight Doc had handed me, and its beam picked up a wicker chair with a ripped-out seat. Then I swung the beam into a far corner; the rough timbers of a wall showed through. There was a scuttling noise.

"Sounds as though this house is already occupied," Doc said.

"You don't scare me that easily." Lucile raised her chin and eyed him brightly.

"The floor looks good," I was saying. It was concrete, pitched to a dry well in the center.

"I think it's hopeless. Why don't you kids live on the houseboat? It would be most romantic." Doc looked at us slyly.

"Now, Bob, you know Lucile can't keep house on a boat. Besides, in cold weather it would be too damp—even for newlyweds."

We all laughed.

"Say, is that a brass lamp?" Lucile said. "It's awfully black." She and Sunny were poking into the pile of junk like two women in an antique shop.

"How about it, Doc? Do you want to let us make it into a house?" I asked.

"Well . . ." Doc's eyes twinkled. "How much will you give me for the contents? Must be a couple hundred feet of lumber stacked up over there, and there's a lot of wear left in those fence posts."

"You're forgetting that Lucile and I will save you the expense of hiring a man to cart this stuff away and demolish the place—unless you were planning to pull it down yourself."

Lucile linked her arm through mine. "Oh, Doc, will you let us—please?"

In spite of Doc's rather negative salesmanship, and the discouraging headshakes of Mamma and Lucile's parents, we took over the garage. An advertisement in the paper brought us a buyer for the houseboat—a GI and his wife paid $2,500 cash and moved right in. Then we spent two weeks cleaning the garage and cutting back the jungle of shrubbery which surrounded it. Then I went to work on the rat tunnels. There were more of them going into the garage than there are railroad tunnels under Grand Central station. I closed up all but one—after all, I didn't want to suffocate the rats under the floor—and started what proved to be a never-ending routine of trap setting.

That was the beginning of our problems.

Fortunately we had many friends.

There was Ray Ninesling, the village chief of police, who possessed many of the qualifications of an architect and a soil expert. Lucile and I relied on his advice to help us with everything from plotting our rough floor-plan to solving the problem of whether the cesspool would drain into Doc Yanover's fishpond.

There was Pop Zuzulo, the house wrecker, who disposed of the by-products of his business in his junk yard. It was a great place to pick up anything from brass pipe to bedroom doors. And Pop knew where to find almost every item he didn't happen to have. He even helped us turn up some new materials. The sheet rock and fiberboard were located in Stamford, part of the plumbing in Port Chester, and the nails came from a ship chandler's shop over in Port Washington. Those galvanized nails with which our house was whacked together will outlast our grandchildren I am sure.

The kitchen sink and bathroom washbowl came from the plumbing shop of Mr. Stasky, a friendly man who had been in business in Great Neck for thirty years. He said he was sorry he couldn't supply the rest of the bathroom fixtures, but I found them in Connecticut and hauled them home in an open trailer behind my car.

We met Mr. Jennings, a builder who gave us plenty of advice on planning and layout; and we also found Bill, the "rough carpenter," in a rooming house in Mineola. He agreed to work on a per diem basis if he was called for and brought home—and, as we later learned, if he was sober.

Pop and Bill spent days rearranging sheet rock in what was shaping up as the living room, and setting up the partitions according to our specifications for the kitchen, bathroom, and a small bedroom. Pop had some important ideas too about how to make certain the stone fireplace I was building in the living room would draw properly.

We were racing to finish the house in time for our wedding in November. One warm day in the middle of the frantic summer, I wiped my forehead on the sleeve of my work shirt and called to Lucile, "Come see my fancy plumbing. I've leaded the last joint."

Lucile, who had been tacking insulation to the walls where I had ripped away the sheathing, came down from her ladder brushing her hands against her dungarees.

We leaned wearily against the same upright.

"It sure is pretty," she said. "When will we know if it works?"

"Mr. Stasky is coming to check it when he sets in the sinks and hot water heater. Of course we can't give the system a final test till the cesspool is dug and this line connected to it."

"What about this piece? Where does it go?" She held up a rectangular slab of marble about a foot and a half long by six inches wide, with a hole in one end.

"I tried all day to figure out where it belonged. When I finally decided, it was too late. It goes right here under the johnnie and I've already cemented it in."

"Let's put it in with the flagstones on the walk by the kitchen door," she said. "We can use it there just as well."

When Mr. Stasky arrived I said proudly, "What do you think of it?"

He shook his head. "Have you ever been a plumber?"

"No, sir."

"Ever worked for one?"

"No." I was feeling less certain about my achievement.

"Do you know what a Y-joint is?"

"Sure." I pointed it out proudly. "This one right here."

"How do you think waste and water will flow through that thing? You've got it reversed."

"I see what you mean," I said. "It was a stupid thing to do."

"As I figure it, you're going to have to throw some mighty educated waste down here to get it flowing the wrong way through that joint, and since you are a very determined young fellow I have no doubt you'll be able to do it."

"Don't be too disappointed in me. Shouldn't I at least get 'A' for effort? I'll make you a proposition. If I sweat out that joint will you put it in right when you set in the rest of the system?"

"I shouldn't." Then he smiled slowly. "Oh, all right."

We had just finished laying the floor in the living room. Bill had worked like a fireball all day, puffing noisily on his pungent pipe and humming and hammering away at a great rate. I had been trying to help him, working along at a slightly more laborious pace. Just as I had hoisted myself to my feet, fighting the overpowering alcoholic glow that enveloped my co-worker, my stumps throbbing with the strain of spending hours in a squatting position, Lucile came up the driveway in the Studebaker.

"It's beautiful," she said. "Darling, we're really going to have a house."

That was all I needed. Bill hummed, puffed, and banged about the room, gathering up his tools and putting them into his kit.

"Well, Bill," I said, "do you approve of the job on the floors?"

He removed his pipe. "She's a damn good floor." He spit noisily into the center of it. "She's a goddamn good floor."

In September the bathroom was finished. While I held the door into the jamb, Lucile set the pins in the hinges and hammered them home from the inside of the room.

"They went in easy," she called through the closed door.

"Hold on while I set the doorknob, then try it." I fastened the screws that held the knob in place. "O.K.—see if it opens," I called to her.

"It's fine—" she peeked through a narrow crack—"except that it won't open any farther. The washbowl is in the way." She started to laugh. "I hope you let me out before dinner."

I had to climb through the window with a chisel to warp out the pins. The next time we hung the door from the opposite side of the jamb.

One day, when I was balanced on a ladder working on the roof, I heard the tooting of a car horn and looked down to see Sunny Yanover waving at me from her convertible, parked in the driveway.

She came over to the foot of the ladder and called up, "Don't come down, Hank. Do you want a dog?"

Since I had my mouth full of roofing nails I could only wave back at Sunny. She told me the story.

It was a thoroughbred Hungarian sheep dog, which belonged to a wealthy family in Port Washington. They could not keep it because one of their children had asthma and was allergic to dog hair. So the Animal League over at Great Neck was trying to find a home for it.

The Yanovers couldn't take the dog because they already had two great Danes, a cocker spaniel, and a cat, but Sunny had immediately thought of us.

"You and Lucile should have a dog, and he has a lovable personality."

I removed the last nail from my mouth and hammered it in. "All right, Sunny, I guess so," I said, more from a desire to get on with the roof than from a conviction that what Lucile and I needed most for our new home was a dog.

An hour later Sunny was back with Chico.

I came down the ladder to meet them. "Which end bites?" I said.

With a slam of the car door, and a slurrp of gravel, Sunny Yanover was off down the road, and I stood eyeing a tremendous, curly, sad-looking, light tan dog. I rubbed his woolly forehead, and he whimpered and licked my hand.

That evening I took him to meet Lucile.

She was impressed—Chico forced this response by sheer size alone.

"This is our first wedding present—from the Animal League of Great Neck. They say he's a puppy."

As the evening passed, we realized that regardless of the provocation, Chico did not bark. Apparently he had never learned how.

The next night before dinner, I sat in the living room with Chico in front of me and a bag of hard candies beside me on the couch.

I held up a piece of candy. Chico alerted himself and reached forward with his head. I drew my hand back and said, "Bark."

No reply.

"Bark—*rff, rff.*"

Chico made a fur-covered whimpering noise and looked at me with imploring brown eyes.

"O.K., fellow, you win." I gave him a lemon drop, which he lapped up gratefully.

Mamma came in from the kitchen. "Who is barking—you or the dog?"

Mamma and Chico became good friends, and in a few days she had him eating and drinking with gusto and he lost his dejected look.

One night as Mamma held up a tidbit for him and said, "Bark, Chico," and I prompted, *"Rff, rff,"* Chico opened his mouth and a clear, sharp, though not very loud bark came out. He looked surprised for an instant, then began running around and around the room, bumping into furniture and jiggling the curtains with his violently wagging tail. When he stopped, he looked first at Mamma, then at me, with a pleased expression.

Then he barked again.

The house-building program put a crimp in my courting activities. I would drive out to Mineola every morning at six, pick up Bill if he was in good shape, then take him to the cottage and work with him till eight thirty when I left for the office. At night I would drive him home, then return to the cottage for a few hours more of work. Saturdays I worked at the cottage all day—it was Bill's day off—then went in to Lucile's house in Washington Heights for dinner.

After one of her father's potent cocktails and her mother's zestful French cookery, I usually succeeded in getting only as far as the nearest comfortable chair before falling asleep. Lucile never complained, although I was not a scintillating guest, and I am afraid I slept away a good many Saturday evenings at her house. In fact, an aunt of Lucile's, who lived in the neighborhood and dropped in often, said to me that day of our wedding, "Hank, it's so nice to see you awake."

I was glad that Lucile decided against a fancy wedding. We were married on November 16, 1946, in her parish church, and Father Antonine, who was then serving in a Franciscan monastery in New Jersey, came to officiate at the ceremony. I was concerned over my inability to kneel during the service, but he merely said, "We won't have any kneeling. I guess the Lord doesn't need you kneeling around here today. Those must be the same Protestant legs you were wearing at Walter Reed."

All of our friends came. A cousin of Lucile's was the maid of honor, and Ed Ford, who was the best man, told me I looked respectably pale as was befitting a bridegroom. After a small reception over in Jersey, Lucile and I drove off in the old Studebaker, which had been scrubbed and polished to the ens, and outfitted for the occasion with new slipcovers. Somehow, a new car would have spoiled everything—it certainly would have wrecked our bank account.

A honeymoon spent in deserted ski lodges in the Green and White Mountains—a tour of New England antique shops in search of old chests and tables we could refinish for the cottage, a visit to Dad Black who had given up the seagoing life and sailed the *Ioneta* up to his brother's farm at Ellsworth, Maine—and Lucile and I went home to set up housekeeping, with a balance of $1.90.

For a salt-water sailor like myself, life in the cottage was doubly romantic. On misty nights there was the reassuring sound of the foghorn at Execution Rocks, and in the early mornings there was the bugling of reveille from the Merchant Marine Academy next door.

As soon as our budget recovered, we began to entertain,

in the manner of most newly married couples. Our weekly dinner guests alternated between friends and our families. Mamma, who had warned me at the start, "You can't take Lucile to live in that garage," told me on her first visit that she had changed her mind about the cottage.

The summer after we were married, Tom Slater left Mutual to go to work for Ruthrauff and Ryan, the advertising agency, on one of the Lever Brothers accounts. He telephoned me one day to ask if I would come to Washington on a temporary assignment to help with arrangements and public relations for the Food Train. Charles Luckman of Lever Brothers was in charge, as chairman of the Citizens Food Committee. I took a leave of absence from Mutual Broadcasting and went to work in Washington with Mike Roche, advertising manager of Lever Brothers, and Drew Pearson, while Tom went out to the West Coast to help get the train started. It would pick up carloads of grain and other commodities donated by communities all the way East. Then the materials were to be loaded onto ships for distribution to war-ravaged countries.

It was a hectic, mad, wonderful existence for the three months it lasted. I was commuting to New York by plane so that I could spend the week ends with Lucile. We were expecting a baby in early March, and her activities were somewhat limited.

One week I came up early and stopped in at the offices of Burlington Mills in New York to talk about a job. One of their vice presidents had heard me speak at the Plaza Hotel before a group of businessmen on the urgent need for the re-employment of veterans in industry. My subject was "Human Engineering." Now they wanted to make me an offer. They were looking for a man to act as personnel director.

The salary was attractive. There were other financial benefits—profit-sharing, bonuses—but best of all the job was challenging.

Lucile and I both liked the sound of it, so I agreed to accept as soon as I could complete my work in Washington and make arrangements to leave Mutual. We told our families about it at our first wedding anniversary dinner at the cottage. Shortly before Christmas, 1947, I started to work at Burlington.

One day in February I was having a conference with a group of engineers in my office in the Empire State Building when Lucile telephoned.

"I'm at Bloomingdale's," she said, "in a telephone booth."

It was unusual for Lucile to call during business hours. Having heard that during pregnancy women sometimes have strange whims, I could only guess that perhaps she wanted me to meet her at five o'clock for cocktails at El Morocco.

Then Lucile said quite clearly, "Hank, I think the baby is coming. What shall I do?"

"Are you sure? But it isn't time yet—"

"Never-the-less—"

"What's the number in the phone booth? . . . Stay right there. Don't go away. I'll call you back."

I buzzed for my secretary. "Get me Parsons Hospital on the phone right away. My wife is having a baby." The engineers sitting around my desk were forgotten.

OB at Parsons Hospital came on the line. "We'll have a bed ready for your wife. Ask the store infirmary to help you. They will call an ambulance if necessary. That will be quicker."

I called Lucile back and repeated the instructions. Her voice sounded weak, but she said, "Don't worry."

In ninety-five seconds I was outside the Empire State

Building hailing a cab that had mercifully pulled up to the Thirty-fourth Street entrance to discharge a fare.

I handed a ten-dollar bill to the driver and said, "This is all yours if you can get me to Bloomingdale's in ten minutes."

"Look, bud, this cab runs on a meter." He pushed the flag down. "Hear that *ticking* noise, like a clock? That's it." He handed back my money as he swung out into traffic.

"Are they having a little fire sale up at Bloomingdale's?"

"No. My wife's having a baby."

The cab spurted ahead suddenly. "Take it easy, bud, this has happened before. Me, I got six kids."

In the days when I was working at Mutual, Tom Slater had broadcast an SOS for Knickerbocker Hospital for volunteer ambulance drivers. The response from listeners had been so poor that Slater volunteered himself, and not to be outdone by my boss, I went along too. I used to wonder then why pregnant women always waited till ten minutes before delivery time before getting the cop on the beat to call the ambulance. Now I was receiving an effective initiation into the unpredictability of the facts of life.

"Here we are, bud. Now I'll sit right here. You go in and find the missus and I'll wait."

"Where's your infirmary?" I charged up to a counter where a girl was tying a scarf around a customer's neck.

In the infirmary I was met by a floorwalker, a store executive, and a publicity man. They all shook hands with me.

"Where is my wife? Is she all right?"

"Quite all right. Our obstetrical nurse is with her."

"I want to get her to the hospital, quick—"

"Before you go in, Mr. Viscardi"—the store executive smiled—"we'd like to tell you that we are prepared to give your wife the best of emergency care. We have an excellent physician on call. If she wishes to stay—and the baby is born here—the store will be proud to present you with a complete layette."

I did not answer. I must get to Lucile.

She reached up from the couch where she was lying and took my hand. The nurse beside her was looking at her watch.

"How are you feeling, honey?"

"All right." But she looked pale.

"How much time is there?" I said.

"An hour anyway, I'd judge," the nurse answered.

We got Lucile downstairs and out to the cab. On the way to the hospital we tried to be scientific while timing the pains, but every once in a while Lucile would giggle. "It might have been fun to have the baby at the store."

"Yeah," said the cab driver, "you'd probably get your picture in the papers."

He got us across the Queensborough Bridge and out to the hospital on time. It turned out that we had five hours to wait before Nina was born.

Our dream cottage now had four occupants. Lucile adjusted her schedule as easily as she had painted and refinished furniture and decorated the house. I passed cigars at the office and did all the wonderful and foolish things a first-time father does. This feeling was something I never could have anticipated. Chico sat on the bedroom floor and watched little Nina's crib by the hour, and got up and tried to put his woolly nose through the bars when she cried. He was distressed because he was not permitted to lick her face.

One day, however, Chico deserted the baby.

"He spent the whole day in front of the fireplace," Lucile said at dinner.

During the evening Chico got up and walked around the room two or three times. Then he lay down, shivering.

"Look, Lucile, his eyes are running. Could he have distemper?"

"He's had shots."

"Let's wrap him in a blanket. Here, old fellow—oh, did I hurt you? There—is that better?"

"You've got a sick dog," the veterinarian said next morning. "His hindquarters are completely paralyzed. He'd better be destroyed."

"What? Kill Chico?"

"It's better than seeing him suffer, isn't it?"

"But isn't there any treatment for this—?"

"It's a canine disease similar to polio. Yes, there is a treatment. It may not be effective."

"Well, let's try it. I'm not going to let a dog die just because he's crippled."

"Give him this medicine—" the vet wrote out instructions —"and apply alternate hot and cold packs to his legs, with massage."

"That sounds like the Sister Kenny method."

"Practically the same thing."

Chico, lying on the table, rolled his eyes upward, but he could not raise his head.

It was a long pull. Under Lucile's careful daily ministrations the soreness left Chico's muscles. By the end of six months he had regained his strength, but the legs were still paralyzed. He would raise himself up on his forepaws and hunch forward, then fall back on his useless haunches, whining. His head would droop to the floor and he would look at us miserably.

One Sunday in the fall I said to Lucile, "I'm going to

make a little cart for Chico. We'll sit his hind legs in it, and rig up a harness, and he can learn to pull himself around."

While Lucile was fussing with the roast I sat at the kitchen table hammering the cart together. There was a cry from the bedroom, and Lucile said, "Nina's awake."

Then she called to me from the bedroom, "Hank—Hank, come here! Quick!"

Something's happened to Nina, I thought, a prayer against a nameless terror rushing to my lips.

In the bedroom, Lucile was holding Nina out in her arms. The baby was reaching a pink hand toward Chico, who stood wagging his tail and looking up at her. He barked and took a couple of steps. He was still dragging one leg, but he was walking!

"He's well, Hank. He's well. He came in here all by himself when he heard Nina cry."

Our dream house was bursting at the seams with happiness. We added another bedroom, for the following May our second daughter, Donna, was born. There was no mad rush to Parsons Hospital this time. Donna came into the world on schedule and quietly. But she has been making up for it ever since.

13

Dr. Yanover's Bill Comes Due

"Director of Personnel Administration" said the Burlington listing in the lobby.

The office was air-conditioned against the New York summer. The marine water color was an original Sessions. My desk was highly polished. The Christmas bonus had been big enough to choke a sheep dog like Chico. My assistants were competent and well groomed. The job was stimulating.

I had built up the personnel department for this growing textile concern from scratch. Throughout the entire organization we now had thirty thousand employees, many of whom I had hand picked. I knew how to find out by careful questioning whether an applicant would be a good company man and, when necessary, whether he was married to the right wife; how to slide smoothly over applicants with physical disabilities.

I looked at my engagement pad. Four interviews with candidates for an executive job. After that I would get to the 1949 wage-revision schedule. Then a labor relations conference. I thought with a sudden sense of guilt that I could be termed a "Successful Young Executive." I still could not believe the figures of my salary—it was good for a man of thirty-seven. Anyone else could do what I had done, though. This was free enterprise. Even my physical disability had not stood in the way. It had been years, in fact, since I had thought of myself as crippled, or even "formerly crippled."

Then Dr. Rusk had telephoned and invited me to have lunch with him today to meet Orin Lehman, a former Air Force captain who was an amputee. "Perhaps you ran into him at Walter Reed," Rusk said. "He was there for two years."

It had been a long time since I had permitted myself to think about the problems of the men I had known so well during the war. Walter Reed seemed like a country I had once visited—a foreign country now that I was safely back home.

Dr. Rusk and his assistant, Jack Taylor, were waiting for me in Rusk's office at *The New York Times,* where he was now an associate editor. The casual friendliness with which Dr. Rusk greeted me gave the impression that he had all the time in the world at his disposal, yet I knew that he was one of the busiest men in New York.

After release from the Air Forces, he had turned his back on his well-established practice as an internist in St. Louis to help reorganize the rehabilitation facilities for both veterans and civilians. His dynamic concept of this new field of medicine had grown into a program designed to help meet the even greater needs of the civilian population. He joined the staff of New York University to head the first department of physical medicine to be established in any medical school. Then he went to Bellevue Hospital, where he was responsible for setting up the rehabilitation wards.

In 1948 he was named director of the Institute of Physical Medicine and Rehabilitation at the New York University-

Bellevue Medical Center. While waiting for construction of
a new building, Dr. Rusk found temporary quarters in an
old structure on Thirty-eighth Street. It had been occupied
by a magistrate's court and had once been a public bath, and
it retained the distinctive features of both. He ripped out
partitions here, put in a gymnasium there, a woodworking
shop here, and the administrative offices there—and made it
serve until the new Institute was opened in 1950.

Rusk had a faculty for assembling just the right experts in
every field—top medical specialists, specially trained nurses,
physical therapists, vocational guidance counselors, skilled
artisans to fashion prosthetics, braces, and wheel chairs. Every
possible device was made available to the needs of his patients—pedal-operated jigsaws, specially designed telephones
and typewriters. He gave them hurdles to overcome in the
form of stairs to climb, rocky paths over which to walk, a
variety of knobs and buttons and levers for the retraining of
useless hands and arms.

He referred to his program as the Bed-to-the-Job concept,
and he was literally proving that patients once considered
hopelessly ill or hopelessly incapacitated could be re-edu-
cated to take their places in society again. Hardly a week
went by without some mention of his dramatic work in the
newspapers.

"Nice to see you, Hank," Dr. Rusk said. "Orin's going to
meet us in the dining room."

By the time the four of us sat down at the table, I liked
Orin Lehman. As had become my habit in the personnel
field, I had sized him up on sight. He was a large-framed
young man, maybe thirty, keen looking. He wore glasses. I
knew something about his background: He was a member of
the prominent banking family, and he had gone with Lehman Brothers' banking house when he was released from the
service. He looked like someone you could trust.

"You should have heard about Hank in Washington, Orin," Dr. Rusk said. "He's the guy who had General Arnold throwing open every key on his squawk-box. The room was jammed with brass in two minutes." Dr. Rusk always kidded me about the day at the Pentagon when he and I had gone to the General's office to get some action for the pilots who were rotting in the amputation wards at Walter Reed.

"Hank," Dr. Rusk said, "Orin has been working on a fascinating project. I'd like to have him tell you about it."

"Well," Orin Lehman said, "it all started with Dr. Rusk's Bed-to-the-Job concept in rehabilitation work. As he says, what is the use of training a man to return to daily life and to a job if no employer will hire him when he leaves the hospital?"

I suddenly remembered rows of men playing pinochle on the sun porches at Walter Reed, who had no desire to leave the shelter of the hospital because they knew what faced them—a life of pension and pity.

"Some time ago we discovered that our program has a weak spot," Dr. Rusk said. "We are getting men on their feet but we're not finding jobs for them."

"Tell Hank about Ernie," Jack Taylor suggested.

"Ernie," Dr. Rusk said quietly, "lost his hands in an industrial accident three years ago. We have fitted him with a set of hooks. He has learned how to dress and feed himself. He can travel alone and is able to take care of all his daily needs. He still has one big need—a job. Ernie has a wife and three small children. He wants to support them."

"Have you the answer for people like Ernie?" I said.

Dr. Rusk replied quickly, "Yes, Orin has, I think. He has formed a committee of young businessmen—Bob Samstag of Stranahan Foil, Jess Stearn over at the *News*, George Simpson and Ray Ripple from IBM, are some of them. They call the group J.O.B.—Just One Break. And they have been interviewing our patients to see what they can do to help them find jobs."

"The younger group is a steering committee," Orin said. "We also have an advisory committee made up of leaders in the community. Bernard Baruch is chairman."

"We've been meeting for about a year now," Rusk said, "and I think we may be on the right track."

"It seems like good grass-roots philosophy," I said. "The problem doesn't lie in any medical agency or government bureau but in the people themselves, in the community—" I stopped. It sounded like a tape recording of something I had said years ago, being replayed through a hollow loud speaker. "Have you—had any luck?" I finished.

"Not much," Orin said. "There's a good supply of labor available now, and the competition is keen. Besides we're learning you can't do personnel placement with your left hand. It's a full-time job for trained people."

"After all," Rusk said, "we are dealing with Big Business—your field, Hank. I think J.O.B. must be set up on a professional basis. By the way, you spent some time researching into the possibilities for the disabled worker in industry, didn't you—right after the war?"

I thought of the halfhearted project I had started and then dropped when Tom Slater offered me a job.

"It was only a beginning," I temporized.

"We're looking for a trained executive director who can take over J.O.B. and run it as a business," Lehman said.

"I think it's a wonderful idea." I was surprised at my enthusiasm.

After lunch Dr. Rusk and Orin Lehman left for an appointment and I went back downstairs with Jack.

"This project sounds interesting," I fished.

"Lehman's a good man." Then Jack filled me in on the details—how Lehman was a high-spirited Princeton undergraduate when the United States entered the war, his hell-bent desire to get into the Air Force. Then he became a forward observer with the Field Artillery, piloting a Piper Cub. He won the Distinguished Flying Cross in the Battle of the Bulge, but he lost a leg before he got back to the States. Army doctors feared they would have to amputate the other.

"He wears a long brace on it," Taylor said.

I remembered noting that Orin walked with the aid of crutches, but the crutches were something you never thought about when you talked to him.

"He's an awfully nice guy. The kind of person you'd like. A little more serious now, according to his friends. Said he had a lot of time to think at Walter Reed. He realized most of the men wouldn't land in a nice family job when they cracked up."

In the taxicab, riding back to my office, I felt like a balloon tire with a slow leak. What's the matter with me? I wondered. This is a great thing. I should feel elated. But the growing emptiness was there. As I left the elevator at my floor, the lavish arrangement of flowers in the reception hall seemed artificial—the colors were too bright. The receptionist didn't look like a real girl—she was much too pretty. And her greeting was much too polite.

This is all wrong, I thought. I'll just have to get out of this mood.

It took a couple of days of the streamlined routine to restore my old sense of values. Wage scales, job analyses, a selection of color swatches to be considered for inserts in the house organ. Life was busy and it was fun, and it could run smoothly if you would only let it.

Then—my secretary's voice: "Mr. Orin Lehman is calling. Will you speak to him? Line two."

The tire went flat. "Hello, Hank." Lehman's voice was friendly, assured. I envied him. It was the voice of a man who is doing something he enjoys. We exchanged pleasantries and he said, "There's something I'd like to talk to you about. Could you make it for cocktails tomorrow—at my place?"

"That's fine. I'd be glad to."

When Orin hung up I jotted a note on my engagement pad and realized that I was not merely being polite. I was looking forward to our meeting.

Orin's man admitted me to his penthouse apartment, on Park Avenue in the sixties. He led me through a large foyer to the library. Opposite, there was a spacious living room and beyond that a terrace where the afternoon sun slanted shadows across the flagstones. One of the French windows was open and a cool breeze was coming in. The room was furnished in good taste, but it was obvious that the library was where Orin spent most of his time.

Bright-jacketed books lined the walls. My host was apparently quite a reader of history and biography. There was a built-in television set, new magazines. I was admiring some framed etchings of boxers when Orin came in.

We shook hands.

"Hank, this is Leonard Elliott. Leonard really runs this place. Keeps his eye on me too. He also makes a good drink. What will you have—Scotch? Martini?"

"Scotch, I guess. With soda, please."

Leonard went out to the kitchen and returned with the drinks. Orin took his on the rocks.

"Cigarette? There are some on that table beside you." He gestured toward a cigarette box and a silver lighter.

There was something strange about Orin's behavior. He was exceedingly polite and yet somehow reticent. Had it not been for the tasteful surroundings and his obvious state of well-being, I would have said his manner was very much like that of a man who had come to my office to ask for a raise. He was almost shy.

His actions were a strange contrast to the collection of candid photographs on the wall, showing Orin at various fund-raising and civic affairs chatting easily with people who regularly made front-page news copy.

"Nice to see you again." He lighted a cigarette.

He so obviously wanted to tell me something, yet did not know how to start that I almost broke into my personnel-director routine of "What seems to be troubling you?"

I concentrated on the highball, from which I took long narrow sips.

"I suppose you think it strange that I asked you to come up," he said.

I raised my glass and watched a small bubble rise to the top. "You don't have to apologize for this. I can't think of a pleasanter way to spend a warm afternoon."

"Well—" he spoke rapidly—"I must admit my invitation was not purely on the social side. I'd like to make you an offer."

"Yes?"

"I realize of course that you may not find it attractive. . . ."

I waited.

"We'd like to know if you would care to head up the J.O.B. Committee."

My mouth dropped open like that of a stage yokel.

Orin went on rapidly. "I realize you're well on your way to success. This is a pretty small endeavor in its present form. And of course it has somewhat limited resources, but I believe in it."

"That's why it will succeed," I said softly. "But as for me—"

"Dr. Rusk and I—and the others—are convinced that you are the man we want for executive director. That is, if you're available. This is a tremendous job. We have absolutely nothing, except the faith of a small group of men who are willing to back an ideal. You've had experience on both sides of the picture. You know the problems of the disabled . . ."

Painful recollections rushed into my mind.

". . . and you know industry's side of the story. It's not too friendly, I'm afraid."

"I hardly know what to say—this is such a surprise. I'm not convinced that I'm the right person for the job, and I'm not sure—"

"I'll admit there's a lot of work to be done. We have no office, not even a typewriter. No administrative organization. But I can give you this assurance: If you come with us, you have my complete co-operation as an individual, and I know I can speak for Bob Samstag and the others."

I realized that I was facing a man who was sold on an ideal. Orin Lehman was not just offering to pick up the check. His enthusiasm was as exhilarating as the good Scotch we were drinking.

Then, suffocatingly, my own uncertainties rushed in. I was emotionally weary, but I strove for cordiality. "It would be untruthful if I said I believed in this any less than you do. Can you give me some time to think it over?"

All the way home on the Long Island Railroad the events of the week clicked by. How had this happened to me? I had clawed my way to a foothold in the structure of business. I was on the way up. The going would be easier from here to the top, now that I had discovered the way. I was a Young Man with a Future. There had been no question in my mind until that luncheon. Now my mind was full of questions.

How far did I want to go? What would I find when I got to the top? Where along the way had I deserted my friends? More than that—my people, the disabled. That wasn't fair, I thought, as the wheels clicked and bumped over a rough bit of track. I had not deserted them. What about all those months during the war when I had taught men to walk, had listened to their troubles, held their hands like a chaplain, and talked to their families?

But what about the years since?

That wasn't fair either. I had no responsibility to others. That had been discharged long ago—except for my family. Could I be blamed for seeking a position with a good financial return? And now that I had found it, why should I give it up? Why trade the security of a top job in a company built on sales, for the distinction of working for an organization built on ideals?

Well, forget about it, I told myself. Call Lehman tomorrow and tell him you can't do it. He'll understand. He would realize that if I had only myself to consider it would be different—but there were others.

Then too—why should I go back to being a cripple? In the security of my air-conditioned job I was a successful young businessman. In the job that Orin Lehman had offered me I would be identified as "that cripple who heads an organization to help disabled people."

Wasn't it asking too much?

But when the train pulled into Great Neck, I was no closer to a decision than I had been at the beginning of the ride. Driving through the summer twilight along the winding roads that led to King's Point, I thought for the hundredth time how lucky I was to live in this semi-rural area. There was air to breathe, and water to sail boats on, and a place for our children to play as soon as they were old enough. I was lucky to have two healthy children, lucky to have two such wonderful neighbors as Doc and Sunny, more than lucky to have Lucile.

Yes, luckier than a lot of people who did not have fresh air and sunshine, and a chance to work at a job they enjoyed.

Luckier than I might have been without some of the people along the way who had helped me—people like Doc.

I owed a lot to Doc, and you couldn't pay it with money. He had never sent me a bill and had been almost shy when I tried to thank him. He seemed to take it for granted, though, that some day I would be able to help someone else as he had helped me.

Just what had I done?

At one time I thought I had succeeded pretty well—that was during the war. But had I? I had gone through the motions of working with the men—only a handful compared to the ones who needed help. I had made the childish error of trying to reorganize the U.S. Army medical team at Walter Reed. I had screamed at the Red Cross and gotten myself thrown out. I had made a halfhearted stab at the industrial problem. Then I had turned my back on the whole thing.

"Daddy—"

"I told Nina she could stay up to say good night to you," Lucile said.

"O.K., little Nina, give me a big hug—how's your baby sister? Good night."

You can seem important to your children even when you are not very much impressed with yourself.

While Lucile and I had dinner on our little porch, we talked over the decision we would have to make—whether I would accept the offer to take charge of J.O.B.

Lucile's first reaction was sure. "I say let's do it. You want to, don't you?"

"Well, let's think it over."

I tried to present the facts: The uncertain financial future, as opposed to my fairly substantial job at Burlington. The fear which I admitted to Lucile of becoming associated again with the disabled. "I don't know whether I have guts enough," I said, reflecting on the long years of feeling like a sideshow curiosity, the frustrations and rebuffs that so often met my efforts to conduct myself like a normal human being.

"I think you are enlarging that fear," Lucile said. "But you're right, you should be sure."

"Frankly, I don't want to go back to being a cripple."

"Hank—" Lucile's face was close to mine—"are you truly happy where you are now? Are you satisfied in the work you're doing? Haven't you pretty much accomplished what you set out to do at Burlington? Where do you go now?"

For a moment she frightened me. Then I laughed. "Of course, I'm happy. In ten more years we'll be riding high. We'll always have the physically incapacitated—you know that—and I'm inclined to let someone else worry about the problem."

"Of course," Lucile said slowly, "you must decide. But I think you're the one to do it. Dr. Rusk expects it of you. It's what Eleanor Roosevelt would expect of you. And it's what Doc would want."

"I'd like to talk to Doc about this," I said.

"There's a light at their place. Let's walk down."

As we sat on the facing sofas in front of the fireplace, I told Doc and Sunny Yanover about the position that had been offered me.

Doc puffed on his pipe, hearing me out. Then he said, "Why should you give up a secure job?"

"I've thought of the same thing, but maybe it's a challenge," I said.

"Challenge is fine, but can you eat it?"

"Oh that," I said. "I need to go on a diet, and Lucile has a light appetite."

"Those bambinos of yours are good eaters," Doc said.

Sunny, who had been silent, now spoke up. "What's all this talk about eating? Everybody knows you have to eat—

the people who offered you this job know it, I'm sure. And maybe it's a job that would bring a lot of personal satisfaction."

Lucile agreed with her. ". . . and I think Hank's the guy to do it."

After we had talked it over for an hour, Sunny turned to me. "I think you're both interested. It's really a case of whether you want to make a financial sacrifice."

"I think you ought to do it." Doc punctuated his unexpected announcement by rapping his pipe on the ash tray beside him. "I believe you want to, and if you really want to then you'd better go ahead."

I still wasn't sure, even after Lucile and I had discussed it late into the night.

We decided to talk it over with Mrs. Roosevelt. Perhaps she could give us a more objective point of view.

A couple of days later Lucile and I spun merrily along the parkway in the direction of Hyde Park, in Sunny Yanover's convertible. Our Studebaker had been to Hyde Park once, but that was some time before, and I did not want to risk its making the long trip again.

Malvina Thompson, whom I had telephoned, had invited us for luncheon at Val Kill Cottage. I told her I had an important matter to discuss with Mrs. Roosevelt.

After a buffet luncheon on the lawn, the other members of the family and the young man who was Mrs. Roosevelt's house guest drifted off, the Roosevelt grandchildren returned to chasing one another in and out of the swimming pool, and Lucile and I were left sitting alone on the terrace with our hostess.

When I told Mrs. Roosevelt about the J.O.B. offer, she immediately asked for details.

"Who else is associated with it? . . . That's good. . . . Isn't it a rather nebulous assignment?"

When she had heard the answers to all her questions, she thought for a few moments, then said affirmatively, "I like the sound of it, Hank. It's something I feel you are particularly well suited for, with your personal background and your experience." Then she turned to Lucile. "What do you think about it, my dear?"

"Well, Mrs. Roosevelt, I'd like to see him take it, if it's really what he wants. But I think he must decide."

"You are wise," Mrs. Roosevelt said.

I probably fitted the job analysis as well as any other candidate. It was indeed a challenge. Perhaps I was going stale in my present work. For example, I could not now for the life of me work up any excitement over an acute labor problem in one of our Burlington warehouses in New Jersey. Lucile and the people who were most interested in me wanted me to do it. But I could not force myself to call Orin Lehman and accept the job.

Something prevented me from doing it. I felt almost as I had that day in Dorsch's shop before I took my first step. Dorsch had said I was ready. I had made all the preparations. Yet I could not move.

The buzzer on my desk sounded. I picked up the inter-office telephone.

"There's an Al Miller outside," my secretary said. "He doesn't have an appointment, but he told the receptionist you would see him anyway."

"Sure, send him in."

Although I had been in touch with Al after leaving Walter Reed, it had been two years since I had seen him. We had gone to a prize fight together at the Garden, when I was working for Mutual.

He limped jauntily across the carpeted floor. "This office is bigger than General Marietta's." His eyes followed the retreating figure of the secretary who closed the door. "Dames, too," he observed.

"Relax," I said.

He slid his long frame into a big leather chair and loosened the collar of his sports shirt. "You've got it pretty soft here—not much like teaching broken-down GI's to walk at Walter Reed."

I flushed at his reminder.

"Say, is it all right for me to be sitting down in your presence?"

"At ease," I said. "Cut out the clowning or I'll beat you over the head with your wooden leg."

"Not this leg." Al brushed at an imaginary piece of lint just above the knee of his flannel slacks. "This leg is a special custom-built job." He swung it over the chair arm.

I winced at the effort I knew was behind this nonchalant gesture, remembering Al's stump that was loaded with shrapnel and covered with skin grafts.

"None of that old peckerwood the Army used to give us. In fact—" he stretched his neck and looked loftily around the room—"I just came in town today for a fitting—at my carpenter's. Fall alterations, you know. On the level, pal, how do you rate this setup? It's pretty classy except for that old bean pot on your desk."

"That's my cooky jar," I said.

"What are you trying to do—bribe the employees with stale cookies?"

"How are you?" I said. "How's your job?"

"Babe and I have *two* kids now, and the job is swell. Still over at the VA on Staten Island. But things aren't so good for some of the other guys. People are fussy about hiring somebody who's been shot up."

"How about the Employment Service? Can't they find jobs for any of them?"

"Are you kidding? They've got veterans hanging from the rafters. I'm lucky I got a break on civil service, but they can't all work for the government."

"I wish I could do something to help." Suddenly it occurred to me that I might appear to be giving Al the brush-off. "Can you have lunch with me?" I said. "We have a lot of things to talk about."

"Can't today, Hank. I'm due at the VA leg factory right now."

As we walked to the elevators I noticed that Al's limp was quite pronounced, but he seemed to be completely undisturbed by it as he kidded me. "Wait till I tell Babe. I never expected to find you in a place like this." Al glanced suspiciously at the heavy carpet.

"Anything wrong?" I said.

"I dunno, just doesn't seem like you. Well, here's my car. See you again, Hank."

"Thanks for coming in today, Al." I shook hands with him. "I'll see you soon."

As I walked back past the pictorial receptionist, I did not attempt to minimize my limp. It no longer seemed important.

Al had broken down the walls of my sham world. There had always been one. The child's world of the hospital, with the insulation of Gouldie's love and guardianship. The world of the block on 101st Street with my mother to keep me safe. The schoolboy's world of the athletes who formed a cordon around me. The world of the cloister where I cloaked myself in the cassock and retreated to the student's carol. The world of the law where I hid inside the identity of Eph Tutt. The world of "a man's war" and my dressing up in a self-styled hero's uniform. The world of success where I poured myself into a stereotype of alert young manhood climbing to the top.

Al's honesty had cut through all my illusions as surely as the shock therapy of his blunt remarks had forced Elaine to face reality that day in the hospital ward. I knew now that I could stop running away. He had shown me the real world, and I must live in it. I must live with myself, not a glorified portrait of a phony superman.

"Get me Orin Lehman," I told my secretary, as soon as I was back in my office.

14

Just One Break

When Orin Lehman told me, "We haven't even a type-writer," he was not exaggerating—there was no typewriter. There was not even a desk to put the typewriter on. Nor an office to hold the desk. We did have one thing though: a file full of applications for jobs.

We had something else too—an active steering committee of young businessmen and a group of leaders in industry who wanted to put the philosophy of J.O.B. to work. They had watched an expanding defense industry absorb the ready labor supply. They had seen statistical proof that the twenty-eight million disabled and overage Americans were a steadily growing factor in our population, increasing at the rate of a quarter of a million a year. They knew that by the year 2000 every worker would be carrying the burden of supporting one of these persons, unless methods were devised through which they could become productive members of society. So it was a case of putting to work individuals classified as "disabled" if our economy were to survive.

We had the human resources and we had the industrial resources. All we needed to do was bring them together. But as I thought about it during the morning and evening train rides and talked it over at luncheons with Orin and Howard Rusk, I realized it would not be quite that simple.

Rusk and others had tackled the problems of rehabilitation. But industry had no specific program to meet it. The safety engineer, the methods engineer, the industrial physician, the personnel director must be brought together into a co-ordinated industrial team to work with the medico-social team and plan for the effective placement of the increasing millions of disabled persons.

Commerce and industry needed an organization to which they could go with confidence as a source of disabled employees and as a laboratory where they could obtain the answer to their placement problems. It was not enough to provide state and federal employment services and the numerous private agencies. A new, special source was needed, the equivalent of a management consultant.

I made some suggestions along these lines at the first J.O.B. steering committee meeting I attended early in November, 1949.

"It seems to me," I said, "that our objective must be to attack the problem from both angles. We've got to persuade management to accept the disabled worker. I don't mean that we should stop trying to place individuals, but if we can change the thinking that's preventing the hiring of these people, then Ernie, the man with the hand amputations, can get his own job."

"How about supplementing that with a broad educational program?" George Simpson said. "Speeches. Newspaper and magazine articles. Radio. Television."

"Do you think you can work speaking engagements into your schedule as J.O.B. director?" Orin asked me.

"You'll have a hard time keeping me quiet," I said. I had given speeches at a few fund-raising affairs for the new Insti-

tute, and found that I was getting the same kick out of
stumping for something I really believed in that I had out
of the rather esoteric "brother's keeper" assignment back in
high school.

"How about invoking the editorial blessing of *The New
York Times?*" I said to Rusk. He smiled.

"While you're changing the thinking on this subject, don't
forget the labor unions," Joe Sullivan, the attorney, broke in.
"You'll need them as well as management to put this program across."

"This is all fine," somebody said, "but the program will
stand or fall on how your candidates handle the jobs."

"We've got to use selective placement," Rusk said.

"That's no real problem," I put in, "with the system you
have of measuring the abilities of your applicants. All we
have to do is fit them into the right slot." I went on: "We'll
proceed slowly. No emotional appeal. No pressure—we'll
send them one candidate at a time. Our people must be so
well qualified that they can't fail."

"And if they do fail—" Bob Samstag looked across at me.
"You can't bat a thousand all the time."

"Then we must stand back of the company. I'd even go so
far as to suggest that we offer to give the exit interview if
our J.O.B. candidate doesn't work out."

I was growing more enthusiastic for this new assignment
day by day as the problems mounted. Many times too I was
assailed by doubts. Was I equal to this test? Could I answer
the challenge of this great work? Aside from its purely economic aspects, J.O.B. had a human side. We were fighting
for more than the survival of a way of life—we were strug-
gling for the survival of human dignity.

If only we could divorce ourselves from the superstitions
in the terminology of disability. The very words were divid-
ing our society, stigmatizing the disabled.

Who are they? The persons with physical disabilities and those who have none are the same in thousands of ways more than they are different. Both are physically limited for numerous occupations and activities of life. Why must we continue to consider the disabled different from other people—to divide our society into sheep and goats?

A really happy man will become aware of his happiness in the course of living twenty-four crowded hours every day. He will not be striving for happiness as a goal in itself. He will be earning it as part of the reward for a full, productive life. No parades, or pensions, or doles, or pity can substitute for the right to support himself and his family in dignity. This priceless liberty cannot be legislated. It must be won by each of us working with all his resources of heart and mind within the limits of his abilities.

There was new interest daily from prominent places in industry. We were building up a strong advisory committee. Allan Lehman, Orin's father; John Hancock, a partner of Lehman Brothers; and I. J. Harvey, president of the Flintkote Corporation, advised that it was sound to get the approval of top management but that we must work through the business channels that were already set up for the hiring of our men and women.

"That's right," Orin said. "A request from the top to put a man to work doesn't always set well with the personnel director."

Then Orin, Bob Samstag and I went to see Bernard Baruch at his home up on East Sixty-sixth Street. We did not have to ask for his blessing—we already had that. The work of the Department of Physical Medicine at New York University had largely been financed by a grant from the Baruch Committee on Physical Medicine, organized after World

War II by Mr. Baruch as a tribute to the memory of his father, a Civil War surgeon.

"My father started this whole concept of physical rehabilitation," Mr. Baruch told us. "Before he died I promised that I'd carry it on."

He listened intently with the famous Baruch hearing aid as Orin brought him up to date on the progress of J.O.B. Then he said, "It's not enough that you do your work here in a single community. You must set up J.O.B. as a pilot program so that the project can be copied by other cities."

As he talked I could see that he thought of J.O.B. in a very wide sense. "It is a big job, but you must co-ordinate the isolated thinking in many places." The faith of this great individual was a challenge—it was encouragement as well.

We further enlisted the aid of Conrad Hilton, the hotel man; Thomas A. Morgan, chairman of the board of the Sperry Corporation; and Bernard Gimbel, president of Gimbel Brothers. And Eleanor Roosevelt was working with us. Her interest in the problems of disabled persons, which stemmed partly from her personal experience in the illness of the late President, had never lagged. Since my contact with her regarding the problems at Walter Reed, and later in industry, I had been personally acquainted with a number of cases where she had been responsible for helping both veterans and civilians who were disabled. No one who sought her aid was ever turned away. It was always an honor to me to receive her request to help another.

J.O.B. was beginning to take shape. We had the advisory committee. We had the vigorous steering committee made up of businessmen, with whom I constantly conferred, either individually or as a group. We had a field to work in. Irving Friedman, who was Dr. Rusk's vocational counselor and right-hand man at Bellevue, helped me to familiarize myself with the rehabilitation wards there.

The first time I entered the rehabilitation ward for men, I was struck immediately with the absence of gloom. Although every patient was incapacitated, many of them seriously, the place was brisk with activity. Wheel chairs came and went between the ward and the rooms down the corridor where the workshops, parallel bars, dining tables, were located. There was laughter, excitement, life. It was the same in the women's ward. Here was none of the resignation that one sometimes associates with the patients in a large city hospital. These people, regardless of their ages, their crutches, their braces, were young in heart. They were ready to live. It gave me a feeling of confidence in the project we were working on.

And while I was becoming acquainted with Bellevue Hospital, I found an office.

It was a maid's room on the eighth floor of the outpatient building. Using a sort of Eph Tutt philosophy, I noted that Dr. Rusk's rehabilitation clinic for outpatients occupied most of the same floor and I asked myself who had a better right to these quarters than J.O.B. We were part of the rehabilitation service, and we certainly were working with outpatients.

The housekeeper gave me the keys on November 30th, and I was in business.

It was a two-by-four, practically under the eaves of Bellevue, but it would do for the time.

Lucile made some curtains for the windows, and we rigged up a screen to hide the washbowl in the corner. We bought a large can of roach powder too, just in case.

Then I telephoned George Simpson at IBM. Yes, he would send me a couple of desks and chairs from one of their warehouses. . . . A typewriter? That could be arranged too. How about some filing cases?

I got in touch with the telephone company, gave them my bank reference, and the following day we had a phone.

Next was a secretary.

Dr. Rusk and I had talked it over and agreed that J.O.B. should be staffed with some disabled workers. I went through the file of applicants. One of them attracted my attention particularly; she had had several years of experience as a stenographer and medical secretary. Struck by a car one snowy morning on her way to work, she had suffered a spine injury. The result was paraplegia. For years she had been a helpless cripple, unable even to turn over in bed. However, she had been retrained in self care and the "Activities of Daily Living" in the rehabilitation wards at Bellevue and now had her own apartment and was ready to return to work in her wheel chair.

Blond and slender, Ann Boyd sat facing me. She was well groomed, and her shiny wheel chair was jauntily upholstered in red leather. I was sold on her from the start.

"How would you like a job as my secretary?" I had outlined the J.O.B. program for her.

Her eyes brightened, and her cheeks were pink with excitement. "I think I'd like it."

"Can you come to my office every day and handle a full-time job?"

"Yes. I've thought it over carefully, Mr. Viscardi. There are two ways I can live my life. One is at home feeling sorry for myself. The other is here, working for you. When do I start?"

But Ann Boyd was not the lucky one. I was. She is the best secretary I have ever had—loyal, devoted, a source of inspiration to me and to all with whom she comes in contact. She was the first of hundreds of persons in wheel chairs who have been placed through J.O.B., and her unsentimental approach to the problems of other disabled persons is as valuable in the working of the organization as is her graciousness in meeting the literal "cross section of society" that finds its way to our office.

The first person who found the office was "Barney," a friendly woman who was one of the Bellevue physical therapists. She won our hearts the first day by bringing us coffee from the little training kitchen next door, where outpatients were helped to relearn domestic skills.

But it was not long before an unending stream of people came. Some of them were derelicts looking for a welfare office. Others thought we were an employment agency. Ann listened to their stories, then tried to direct them to the place where they could get help. We had to explain to the disabled persons that we could only assist them if they were referred to us through Dr. Rusk's rehabilitation program. There were two reasons for this: When he turned over a job applicant he gave us a complete medical, psychological, and vocational report, the most comprehensive measure of a person possible. The second reason, always a sad one, was that we had far more applicants than we could handle with our limited staff.

But, one by one, we were placing J.O.B. candidates in jobs. And we did it by measuring, not their disabilities, but their abilities to meet the demands of the job—physical and otherwise.

Sylvia was a beautiful girl. Polio which caused muscular involvement in both legs and one arm had not affected her warm personality. She was trained as a switchboard operator at Bellevue and from there we sent her out on a regular job.

Frank, a GI who had lost an arm in Germany, went to work as an accountant at the Plaza Hotel. His placement was worked out in the classic J.O.B. pattern with Bernard Baruch talking to Conrad Hilton, owner of the Plaza, then various interviews set up by members of the J.O.B. steering committee. Before we finished, we had even brought Dave Herman of the Hotel and Club Employees Unions into the picture. Charles Chiusano, personnel manager of the Plaza, became a member of the steering committee. And Frank got the job. He became the first of a series of applicants we succeeded in placing as telephone operators, doormen, elevator men, and kitchen helpers in hotels throughout New York City. To Frank it meant the first step toward buying the home in the country he wanted, a chance to be a real father to his three children.

Then there was Joe, the stevedore. While working in the hold of a ship, his legs had been crushed by a heavy crate. He wanted to go back on his crutches to the smell of the docks and the rough life he had known. Analysis of the jobs available showed there were three or four he could handle. But getting in touch with his union was another thing.

When I telephoned Joe Ryan, president of the International Longshoremen's Association, his conversation was not exactly couched in diplomatic language and ended with me looking into a buzzing receiver. So I drove down to Pier 61 in the Hudson River, hoping to locate Eugene Sampson, business agent of Local Union 791. He was harder to see than the President of the United States, and remembering my failure to reach the heart of Mr. Ryan, I abandoned more and more hope with each rebuff from a husky dock-side lieutenant. But finally I passed the last one and was shown into the office of a very friendly, intelligent man. Gene Sampson and I might have been chatting over lunch at the Biltmore.

He listened to my explanation of J.O.B., and when I told him about Joe, he said, "Send him down tomorrow. We'll put him to work as a checker."

As I was leaving, he said, "Let me know whenever I can help you." He has been an unofficial member of the J.O.B. family ever since.

When it came to finding a job for Ernie we had to sell management.

Ernie Della Donna was introduced to the J.O.B. steering committee at one of the monthly Thursday meetings at Bellevue Hospital. He sat at the table and smoked a cigarette with one of his prosthetic hooks as he answered the questions put to him. He explained that he wanted to return to working in an industrial plant as he had been at the time of his injury, when a hydraulic press crushed his hands and they were amputated above the wrists.

The report on Ernie in the folder before each committee member indicated that he was fitted to perform a number of jobs, that he was quick and receptive to training, that he had run errands and worked as a file clerk, as well as helped to train other arm amputees in the Activities of Daily Living program at the Institute of Physical Medicine and Rehabilitation.

After some discussion of placement possibilities, one of the committee members, Bob Lea of the Sperry Corporation, spoke. "You know, Hank, I'd like to try to place Mr. Della Donna out at the Ford Instrument Division of Sperry. Maybe he could be our first man there. We're going out on Thursday to see them."

It sounded like a possibility.

The meeting with the executives of Ford Instrument started off in an unfavorable atmosphere. Dr. Benjamin Berg, the plant medical director, was opposed to J.O.B. and made his position quite clear.

"Mr. Viscardi is going to ask us to hire disabled persons. I say we have enough cripples in our plant now—we don't need any more."

"Dr. Berg," I said, "what is a cripple?"

As we talked, it developed that his concept of a cripple

was someone who might drop dead at his workbench, an employee who might have an epileptic seizure while working on a machine and threaten the safety of others, or, say, a blind man who might get in the way of a moving crane.

"What I must do is protect our company from increased liability," he said.

I explained that, properly placed, a disabled worker brought no increased liability. Then I mentioned Ernie. "Do you feel that in a job that is geared to his physical abilities Ernie would be a liability to your company?"

"Well, perhaps not," Dr. Berg said. "I'd have to think about it."

"Casualty insurance companies specifically recommend the employment of disabled persons, because they are sound risks," I said.

Then I told the other staff members that we wanted to represent them. "We don't want to send you anyone who is not going to do a good job. We'll even give the applicant periodic medical checkups—say every six weeks, if you'd like. What we want to do is send you one man as a test case."

"In that event, gentlemen," Dr. Berg said, "I withdraw my objection. Under the conditions Mr. Viscardi has mentioned I'm willing to go along with this trial case."

The result of the meeting was that Ford Instrument agreed to interview Ernie. The job we decided on was as a helper in the experimental division, where he would keep records, bring materials and tools to other workmen, and clean machines.

We analyzed the job carefully and Ernie was completely job-tested at the Institute. One of his tasks would be to lift a box containing instruments from a workbench and place it on a dolly. The maximum weight of the box would be forty pounds. So, as part of his training, Ernie was taught to lift a similar box weighing sixty pounds.

We went into the company cafeteria, investigated the problems that might give Ernie trouble—moving his tray through the line, paying the cashier, etc.—and worked out solutions involving the minimum of difficulty to himself and delay to his fellow workers.

The day Ernie came to our office to report on his final interview and physical examination, I knew without asking how it had turned out.

"I start Monday," he said.

This was the beginning of a new life for Ernie Della Donna. At last he would be able to support his wife and children.

"Ernie," I asked, "did you run into any trouble during the interview?"

He smiled ruefully. "Yes, one little thing—when I went in for my physical. You know, I still can't handle the small buttons on my shirt with these things—" he looked down at his two hooks—"but it was all right. Dr. Berg helped me unbutton them."

People were beginning to hear about J.O.B. There were Dr. Rusk's articles in the *Times*. Eleanor Roosevelt devoted a column to it, and Tex and Jinx McCrary did a series in the *Herald Tribune* in addition to having us on their television show. Then there was an article in *Collier's* magazine by John Conner. Journals of medical and philanthropic societies picked up the idea. We were gradually being publicized in house organs and industrial magazines. Then after the Institute of Physical Rehabilitation and Medicine moved to its new building at First Avenue and 34th Street, in January, 1950, the *Saturday Evening Post* published a dramatic story by Joe Alex Morris, depicting the center which was fast becoming a model in cement and glass for rehabilitation centers all over the world. A good part of the article was devoted to the work of J.O.B.

After the *Collier's* article appeared, letters flooded in in such quantities that the girls had to parcel them out and take them home nights. By this time I had a new assistant. She was Alfrida Burnette, a sympathetic and intelligent woman who wanted to work on a voluntary basis. When I learned of her background as a private secretary in a large business office and her more recent work as a volunteer, teaching typing to the patients in Bellevue's rehabilitation wards, I offered her a job.

"Volunteer help is fine," I said, "but I need a full-time assistant."

Mrs. Burnette is the kind of person who can sit and listen patiently to the labored telling of a truly hard-luck story. She can spend an afternoon of relentless telephoning. She can discuss placement problems with a prominent business executive. She can analyze a job and gauge a candidate's potential for it. She can help set up a television show or act as hostess to a group of out-of-town dignitaries. And she never loses her self-possession or her charm.

Though the letters were as varied as the types of places they came from, we discovered they fitted into half a dozen categories. If people wrote to inquire about employment or vocational training, we referred them to local agencies. Letters from prisoners in state institutions and patients in mental hospitals were handled carefully too. But some of the oddest letters came from people who were not patients in mental hospitals—people whose warped drives found inarticulate expression in almost illegible writing, people with strange feelings of persecution or inventive minds. A completely illogical idea for a new crutch, or a shoe that could be put on and off without lacing. All were sifted and answered. The mash notes we threw away.

People hammered our doors down. Our telephone was as busy as we. One morning when I arrived at work, Ann said we had had a telephone call from a place up in the Bronx. "They would like to hire disabled people as unskilled labor."

"Usual setup?" I said.

"Yes. Third-floor walk-up. Sounds like a sweatshop. Twenty-eight dollars a week. They cooled off when I told them to write us a letter and we would investigate."

"Good girl. Anything else?"

"Yes," Mrs. Burnette said, "I got one almost as bad. Somebody wanted a one-armed man to sell spices from door to door."

"Oh yes—" Ann handed me a letter—"this came in today."

The writer wanted "a disabled veteran who has been overseas and has a leg missing, to work in a responsible job in our organization."

"Write to them, Ann, and ask them if it makes any difference whether he lost his leg in a lawnmower or had it shot off. Tell them he still needs a job just as badly. I'll sign it— Never mind. I'll talk to him on the phone."

Our education program was progressing as well as could be expected. Dr. Rusk was always speaking somewhere and Orin Lehman and I appeared at service clubs, industrial groups, nurses' and medical associations. The more speaking engagements we filled, the more requests we received.

Dr. Rusk and I attended the monthly dinner of the Office Executives Association of New York, which had members from eight hundred companies. After we finished speaking, they voted to set up their own J.O.B. committee. Working with this group served as a springboard to many important activities.

Interest came too from the war veterans. The New York City Advertising Men's Post of the American Legion voted to set up a J.O.B. wing. In doing so they indicated that their objective was not confined to assisting veterans with service disabilities, but extended to helping those who had survived the war without casualty and later became incapacitated through illness or injury.

Probably the most gratifying reaction was the inquiries that began to filter in from other cities and states asking for advice about setting up a J.O.B. type of program. We began to fill speaking engagements all the way from Montreal to Knoxville, Tennessee.

The community of Knoxville faced a serious problem. There was a labor shortage which might become grave as defense industries expanded. Besides, the city was over-burdened with welfare costs for the support of the disabled and their families. Business and social agencies got together with the help of Hank Smith, director of the Tennessee Division of Vocational Rehabilitation, and Miss Mary Switzer, national director of the vocational rehabilitation program, and organized "Operation Knoxville," a project to get people off relief and back to work.

I was invited down to speak at a luncheon meeting of government officials and representatives of various community organizations. We discussed the problems and their solution—and the result of this meeting was that a permanent community organization was set up. One of its active divisions is a J.O.B. committee.

What they learned in Knoxville proved to be an irrefutable argument in favor of the J.O.B. philosophy. Knoxville had five hundred families on relief because of the disability of the wage earner. This was costing the taxpayers $325,000 every year. The investigation showed that the cost of rehabilitating two hundred and fifty of these family wage-earners would be $113,000, a one-time expense. This would save the community more than $160,000 a year, and those rehabilitated workers would return approximately $400,000 of new wealth to the community every year and would be happier friends and neighbors.

Besides the growing interest in employment of the disabled in local areas, there was evidence of new interest on a national scale when in 1951 the Office of Defense Mobilization set up the Task Force on the Handicapped to make a thorough study and recommend specific procedures. The group was composed of representatives from the fields of medicine, sociology, industry, labor, and personnel placement. I was invited to serve, as director of the J.O.B. committee.

Again I was traveling to Washington—not the Washington of the frustrating and exhausting Walter Reed days, but the Washington of the Luckman Committee and the Food Train. I felt right at home spending two or three days at a time in the Lafayette Hotel, where I had lived before. It felt good again to walk across Lafayette Park mornings, past the White House where the Citizens Food Committee had worked, and on to the unbelievably honeycombed old State Department Building. This was where we met. From these leading citizens with whom I was privileged to work, representing all parts of the country, came an inspired American solution to the problem.

In the report which the commission published in 1952, we stressed the fact that the employment of the physically incapacitated was a problem of long standing, rather than of an emergency period, and would require a long-range solution. We recommended that it be worked out not by a specific agency but by the utilization of all the facilities of the community, by the setting up of committees of medical and vocational experts, leaders of industry and labor.

Actually, the report paralleled the lines of the J.O.B. philosophy.

As my second year with J.O.B. progressed, it was becoming apparent that we would soon outgrow our one-room office. Unfortunately the new Institute was using every square inch of its architectural perfection for the care and treatment of its patients, so that all we could garner there was a desk where I interviewed Institute patients and parked my brief-case when I attended evaluation clinics. At these clinics the patient was introduced to the Institute staff, his own hopes for rehabilitation discussed, and recommendations made by department heads. It was an inspiration to watch this new concept unfold—that of treating the whole personality, not just the amputation or the illness.

It is not enough to treat the illness. The whole man must be treated, including his psychological reactions to his dis-ability and his learning to live and work with what he has left. Medical science in most instances cannot restore de-generated nerves and make dead limbs useful and powerful again. It can, however, give to people the opportunity to live the most useful, happy lives of which they are capable, to live not only within the limits of their disabilities but to the hilt of their capabilities. This was Dr. Rusk's final phase of medical care, taking the patient from the bed to the job. J.O.B. was providing the final step of a dynamic new pro-gram. Without it there was no cure, only frustration and disillusionment: to be rehabilitated to idleness in a wheel chair or on crutches, instead of in an invalid's bed.

Our search for a new location ended when the Bellevue switchboard outgrew its quarters on the first floor of the administration building and we were assigned to the space. The new office was central, easily accessible to visitors from outside, and much closer to the rehabilitation wards than our former one.

Ellen Lehman McCluskey, Orin's sister, who had been most generous in her support of J.O.B., volunteered her services as a professional interior decorator, and transformed the institutional-type rectangle into what we modestly refer to as the most attractive office in New York.

"Ellen," I told her as my voice bounced back and forth across the white-walled room, "I have big plans for this place."

"Let's hear them."

"The people who come here looking for jobs have spent years in hospitals. Nothing about J.O.B. should suggest a clinic where doctors and social workers are going to hold their hands. I want it to look like a business office, a place where they will feel that they are on their own. Yet I want it to be warm and attractive."

"I understand." Her eyes were detailing the office as her mind created a new setting. "How about that glass and wood partition?"

"As far as I'm concerned it can stay. That room at the end is just about the right size for my private office. But I wish the partition weren't so ugly."

"We'll fix that."

Ellen and her assistants went to work, and for a couple of weeks there was a flurry of painters, designers, swatches of fabric, and samples of paint.

When the last block-printed linen curtain (made for us by the Bellevue housekeepers) was hung, the place was transformed. The too-long windows had been shortened by installing cornice boards. Unsightly radiators were boxed in. Both offices, including the partition, were painted a deep blue-green. A magazine table was designed to fit an awkward jog in the wall of the reception room. The chairs, upholstered in two shades of green leather, were comfortable and easily accessible.

Ellen suggested bright modern paintings for the walls. One which causes considerable comment from visitors is a framed original textile design by Rose Hiraga, a quadriplegic. Her back was broken in an automobile accident and she suffered partial paralysis of both arms and legs as a result. Many of the other paintings were done by former patients, like Gilbert Provencher, who broke his neck while driving and now works with his brush held in a leather cuff on his elbow, while he rests his useless hand on his shoulder.

"I'm all through with your office," Ellen said. "You add the personal touches."

Lucile and I took over from there.

"I've found just the picture for this wall," Lucile said. "It's a Gordon Grant water color. You can sit all day and look at sailboats." (The Sessions painting from my Burlington Mills office had been promoted to the spot over the fireplace at the cottage.)

The desk lamp had a base made from a brass ship's lantern we had found in Doc's garage before converting it. I hung a miniature portrait of Lucile and the two children beside my desk, and set a model of a schooner on the recessed window ledge. The cooky jar from Burlington was installed within reach of everybody.

In August, 1951, we moved into these offices, along with our files which had by that time expanded into half a dozen large cases. But many of the applications they held had become inactive—because the people had jobs.

There were people like Bob, the clean-cut Harvard kid with an M.A. in business administration. The main difference between Bob and his classmates was that, in addition to being above average scholastically, Bob was blind. He had taken a secretarial course too—more than anything else he wanted a job. After a few weeks under Mrs. Burnette's supervision in the J.O.B. office, where he answered the telephone and conducted interviews with poise and charm, Bob was hired as secretary to a prominent investment banker.

There was Laura, a thin, brown-eyed sparrow of a girl the first time I visited her in the wards at Bellevue. Polio affecting both legs, plus neglect by a family which felt a sense of shame in having a cripple in the house, had deprived her of education and the opportunity for social development. One day she fled from home and was directed to the rehabilitation wards by the sisters at a Catholic charity.

The last time I visited Laura at the hospital I took her a present. The gift I drew from my pocket was a Social Security Card. Her brimming eyes were hard to face. Shortly after that she was hired by a company manufacturing novelty greeting cards. Her first job was pasting feather tails on Easter ducks. She did it so well that by the end of seven months they promoted her to a supervisor's job—she was such a rapid worker that she threw the assembly line out of balance. At the end of a year she came back to visit us, wearing a new Easter hat and suit she had bought with her own money. "You're beautiful, Laura," I said. Her big eyes sparkled. She didn't look like a sparrow any more.

There was Mr. Wilson, the man with cerebral palsy who had studied for the ministry. After graduating from the seminary he was told that he could not be ordained, since, though a man of high intelligence, he had great difficulty in speaking. He had had just two assignments—one in a backwoods community where he finally had to admit that he could not live on the salary of twenty-five dollars a month, the second in a boys' reformatory where poverty and institutional pressures had finally proved too much for him.

He agreed that the nature of his impairment was a severe drawback in his work, but he had his heart set on serving in some capacity in the church. We were not able to find him a job of this type, although we even tried to place him in a theological library. I was reluctant to send him out into the business world for fear that his lack of interest would result in failure. So I arranged with two business acquaintances to see him. One was the personnel director for a large metropolitan newspaper, the other for a sales organization. They talked to Mr. Wilson as though they were giving a routine job interview, then reported back to me. "Don't worry about this man's being unhappy in a job that is away from the ministry," they said. "He's hungry, and he wants to work." Shortly after that we were able to guide Mr. Wilson to a position in the advertising department of Allied Stores. He is still there.

Here is a young man with a fine mind and radiant spirit and no trace of bitterness. With severe involvements of speech, gait, and movement, he is disabled physically but not industrially. Comparing him with another worker in the advertising department of Allied Stores, you might conclude that one is disabled and the other is not. Yet neither is disabled for the particular job he is doing, and both are disabled—that is, lack physical or other qualifications—for many other jobs. What we are comparing are two "disabled" persons neither of whom is really disabled for the job he is satisfactorily performing.

In the long reception room of our new offices we set up a small switchboard and four desks, and two more young women joined our staff.

Westray Boyce, a college graduate who had majored in philosophy and psychology, came to see me one day and said she would like a job with more challenge than the one she had in the personnel department of an insurance company. This intelligent young woman became a personnel assistant. She has not only been quick to learn the requirements of industry, she has a facility for getting along with the varied personalities with whom we deal, and she possesses a wide range of skills—she can run a 16-millimeter sound movie projector as easily as she can prepare a financial statement for a meeting of the J.O.B. steering committee.

Terry Turrigiano, who was a patient at Goldwater Memorial Hospital, had been fighting a six-year battle from wheel chair and bed against the advances of rheumatoid arthritis, when the revolutionary benefits of ACTH were discovered. She was one of the earliest patients treated with this drug. In three months she was discharged from the hospital and taught to give herself her regular injections. Shortly afterward she came to work for us as a clerk and typist. "This is my first job in six years," Terry said. Although one arm and one leg are affected by arthritis, Terry's perkiness and charm and her ability to handle a physically tiring job are not affected one bit.

The staff was almost complete, a group that lived its work. It was a privilege for me to be part of such a team with Howard Rusk and the others.

In the fall of 1951 the Board of Education invited us to participate in a television show which they were producing for high school students who were hospitalized or homebound because of disability. The show, televised three mornings a week over WPIX, was devoted to academic subjects for which the students received credit when they had written the Regents' examinations, and to vocational guidance with a view to helping them after graduation.

This was where we came in. Our segment of the show, which was televised every Wednesday, was to be called "Make It Your Business." I fell in with the plan enthusiastically, and found myself reliving some of the old days at Mutual Broadcasting, especially since I called on Tom Slater for advice. Once again there was the excitement of working out the script, of inviting people to be on the show, of living by the stop watch and the "on the air" signal. This time there was something new—the eye of the camera.

The series for which we contracted ran from October 15 to March 1. We tried to give the disabled young people who might some day enter industry a perspective that would help them find jobs. I acted as host and interviewer. The programs were varied—one week maybe we would set up a J.O.B. steering committee meeting, at which we would introduce persons with physical disabilities who were looking for jobs. Another time, through motion pictures, we would take the audience inside a busy metropolitan bank for a chat with the personnel manager, a tour of various departments with special attention to the kinds of jobs incapacitated persons could fill, and a close-up of a disabled worker who was on the bank staff. One program was devoted to a series of interviews between a personnel director and job applicants—pointing up the right and wrong approaches. This show stressed the importance of our audience competing with workers who had no outstanding impairments, the necessity of being available on time five days a week and not expecting special favors.

Other shows illustrated special devices and equipment for the use of disabled workers and jobs for beginners. Programs were also planned to help orient them to the attitude of the community and the over-all picture of their place in industry. Through the co-operation of business we televised many fields—the dress industry, advertising, the hotel business, instrument manufacture.

Personalities appearing on the show were varied—an industrial leader, a beautiful blind girl secretary with her seeing-eye dog, a young man in a wheel chair who held an administrative job, an office worker with an artificial hand, a minister and his wife both of whom were blind.

It was indeed an added burden of responsibility preparing script and appearing in a half-hour television show each week. Its returns in encouragement to the disabled youngsters for whom it was intended were more than adequate. The surprising result was the volume of mail we regularly received from adults and business people who found it a source of inspiration.

In the spring of 1952 the Associated Press did a series of feature articles on J.O.B. and Sidney Fields devoted two columns in the New York *Mirror* to us. As a result we received a request from the Kate Smith TV show to let one of our J.O.B. applicants appear. We had just the man for them.

Harry was in his late twenties. He was introduced anonymously on the show as a representative of two million disabled workers seeking jobs. Stricken with polio in 1942, shortly after he had passed his Navy physical, Harry fought his war in an iron lung while his buddies from his baseball team were called to Europe and the Pacific. Years in hospitals and rehabilitation centers brought back the functions of his arm and chest muscles. His legs remained impaired, but that did not prevent him from working from his wheel chair as a draftsman in a war plant. Later he won a scholarship to college where he managed the campus radio station and was assistant manager of the football team. He majored in psychology and got good grades. You couldn't talk to Harry for more than a few minutes without being aware of an outgoing sense of humor and an alert mind. Nevertheless, he had been looking for a job for six months. Employers were prejudiced against the wheel chair.

The next time we get such a request we won't be able to send Harry—he's working now. A farseeing business leader hired him for on-the-job-training shortly after the show.

Then there was the movie.

It had started one day soon after we were settled in our new quarters. Ann Boyd wheeled smartly into my office and announced a visitor. The businesslike young woman introduced herself as representing the Reorientation Branch of the U.S. Army.

"We make educational films," she said.

Then she explained the purpose of her visit. The Army was doing a series of documentaries on American life for export to Japan, and they thought our project would serve as the basis for an interesting film. "We want to show them a good example of democracy in action. Your movement as American businessmen seems like a good one. Perhaps we can portray the complete rehabilitation of one patient, and his return to a job."

"That sounds like a good idea," I said. "We can give you hundreds of cases . . ."

The man they selected was a husky young coal miner named Charlie Moore. When he was in his early twenties his back was broken in an accident at work, paralyzing him from the waist down. Charlie was bedridden for ten years. Then one day the United Mine Workers Welfare Fund offered to send him to the Institute for Physical Medicine and Rehabilitation in New York.

He was a personable young man, and he was willing to play his own role in the movie. The new Institute made a perfect setting and the early scenes in the film were shot in an actual mining town in Pennsylvania.

Charlie's progress from Bed to Job was dramatically portrayed, with all the resignation of his wasted life, then the glimmer of hope, the trip to New York, the hard work and disappointments of the first exercises for strengthening arm and upper-back muscles, the frustrating experience of trying to learn to walk again with parallel bars and braces and crutches, the failures, then little by little the successes. Then Charlie's discovery and development of his talent for painting and drawing in the Institute workshop, and finally the day he left the hospital in his wheel chair en route to his new job as a letterer and silk-screen operator in a printing establishment.

The film was titled *A New Beginning*, and it had its preview at a cocktail party at Toots Shor's restaurant in February, 1952. All of our friends were there—two or three hundred of them. It was a great occasion when people interested in rehabilitation and in J.O.B. could come together.

At the end of the showing, Dr. Rusk announced: "This story has a heroine as well as a hero," and he introduced Charlie Moore and his wife. Mrs. Moore was the head nurse of the miners' ward at the Institute when Charlie became a patient there, and they were married when he was discharged from the hospital.

But if only the picture could have told all of the other wonderful things about Charlie Moore: the wasted years when he rotted abandoned and forgotten in a mining town, living with no purpose or hope; how he went to night school to study free-hand lettering and silk-screen painting; how we placed him in a job as a disc jockey—"New York's Wheel Chair Disc Jockey," the newspapers had called him, this man who had been a coal miner since childhood and had a bare minimum of education.

If the picture could have told of the boundless love of Gertrude Moore, which allowed her to find her destiny with this man whom the world would always consider different. If it could have told how the understanding of an American community nourished that love, believed in it, provided Charlie Moore with an opportunity to support himself and his wife in dignity. If it could have described the quiet cottage on the Jersey Coast where they now live close to his work.

Could this enduring love be a lesson to all the communities of America? Could it help us achieve understanding to overcome the superstitions and backward psychological reactions toward disability, to look upon all persons as truly God's children, and not divide humanity into the blessed and the damned?

The J.O.B. philosophy was only beginning to catch on. True, organizations were springing up in other communities: Knoxville, Chicago, Hartford; Bergen County, New Jersey, and Westchester County, New York; Philadelphia, Montreal, and Mineola, Long Island. One by one, industrial firms were beginning to work with us as they realized the necessity of utilizing all the employable skills available in the community if the economy were to stand.

But our work would never be finished. Ancient aversions were still aflame. Too many of us are shocked by disability. At least no ordinary person admires deformity. We find relief many times in sympathy and tolerance. This is but a pleasant compensation for more complex feelings which are difficult to admit honestly, and harder to change.

On the other hand, the disabled do not want special favors. Some disabled people in whom I have put my trust have disappointed me. There have been rich rewards even in this experience, for it has proved that they are not different from other people.

If we can only get more people thinking along the lines of *ability* rather than *disability*. All of us are physically limited. It is just a matter of degree. Steeled in the crucible of suffering, many of the disabled have developed compensatory qualities to offset the extremes of physical makeup. We must think in positive terms—first, of a person's *abilities* and second, of helping him to utilize those abilities to the fullest extent in living his life. It is a case not of matching a worker to a job, but of seeing both the job and the worker as entities that constantly change and readjust. This concept of utilizing all available industrial and human factors can work for the benefit of everyone—the employer, the worker, and the community.

If we can only see with the vision of true love that Gertrude Moore possessed, and discard the negative labels. Charlie was not a paraplegic. He was a man—the man she loved. He was a worker—productive, happy. Let the doctors and the people in professional rehabilitation circles use the terms that excite superstition. We should not even use the word "handicapped." The appropriate words are "man" and "woman." Human beings.

One of the people I most wanted to have at the preview could not come—Dr. Yanover. He was delayed by an emergency operation at Parsons Hospital. But he did arrive in time to have dinner afterward. As Doc, Sunny, Lucile, and I sat around the table with Charlie and Gertrude Moore, I reflected that the happy ending Dr. Rusk had postscripted to the film was truly a "new beginning" for Charlie and his wife. Doc had made a new beginning possible for me a long time ago. And he had told me to try to make the difference to another life. How many more people were waiting to be helped to live their lives anew?

It would be a long time before J.O.B. was set up in every town, alongside the church and the post office, as a permanent institution accessible to everyone in the community. But we could not let that deter us. We could not let down the millions of Charlie Moores who were still waiting.

It was a rough road ahead. But it was a road that went somewhere.

Lucile quietly put her hand in mine. I believe she knew what I was thinking.